# Praise for *The Top 50 Management Dilemmas*

'I thought the book was an incredible tool to have at your fingertips. I found that all the management dilemmas that I have come across were covered and were easy to access. I could really see how I would continue to use it as a reference guide rather than let it gather dust in my drawer like so many of the books on management that I have read.'

**Mark Eastham, Multi Channel Director, Carphone Warehouse**

'This is a well-written book which does what it says on the tin! There is no doubt that this book provides a great reference text when you face a management challenge and (whilst it might not solve your dilemma!) it will certainly point you very much in the right direction.'

**James Percival, Vice President, Operations Finance EMEA, Hilton Worldwide**

'At last a management book that is full of practical advice not theory! To be a successful manager you need to understand people and how you interact with them. This book deals with challenges we all face and gives useful advice to assist us in improving our people management skills.'

**Brian May, Chief Executive, Renew Holdings Plc**

# The Top 50 Management Dilemmas

# The Top 50 Management Dilemmas

Fast solutions to
everyday challenges

**SONA SHERRATT AND ROGER DELVES**

**PEARSON**

Harlow, England • London • New York • Boston • San Francisco • Toronto • Sydney
Auckland • Singapore • Hong Kong • Tokyo • Seoul • Taipei • New Delhi
Cape Town • São Paulo • Mexico City • Madrid • Amsterdam • Munich • Paris • Milan

PEARSON EDUCATION LIMITED
Edinburgh Gate
Harlow CM20 2JE
United Kingdom
Tel: +44 (0)1279 623623
Web: www.pearson.com/uk

First published 2014 (print and electronic)

ISBN: 978-0-273-79284-0 (print)
       978-0-273-79469-1 (PDF)
       978-0-273-79470-7 (ePub)
       978-1-292-00847-9 (eText)

*British Library Cataloguing-in-Publication Data*
A catalogue record for the print edition is available from the British Library

*Library of Congress Cataloging-in-Publication Data*
Sherratt, Sona.
   The top 50 management dilemmas : fast solutions to everyday challenges / Sona
   Sherratt and Roger Delves.
      pages cm
   Includes index.
   ISBN 978-0-273-79284-0
   1. Management. 2. Supervision of employees. 3. Decision making. I. Delves, Roger.
   II. Title.
   HD31.S448 2014
   658–dc23
                                    2013029663

10 9 8 7 6 5 4 3 2 1
17 16 15 14 13

Cover design by redeyoffdesign.com, image © mypokcik/Shutterstock.com

Print edition typeset in ITC Giovanni Std by 3
Print edition printed and bound in Great Britain by Henry Ling Ltd, at the Dorset Press, Dorchester, Dorset

NOTE THAT ANY PAGE CROSS REFERENCES REFER TO THE PRINT EDITION

For David, who always believes. And for Jess, Sophie and Arabella, may our hands always be intertwined together.

For C and for three magic monkeys – my electricity.

# Contents

# 2 Challenges with teams

# 3 Challenges with externals

# 4 Challenges around conflict

# 5 Challenges around change

# 6 Challenges around power, politics and influence

# 7 Challenges for yourself

# About the authors

**Sona Sherratt** has been an Ashridge faculty member since 2003. She designs, teaches and client directs on various tailored executive programmes with clients such as SABMiller, Avis, Erste Group Bank, Renew Holdings and Continental Automotive Group. She teaches on various open programmes including the Ashridge Leadership Process, Influencing Skills and Strategies and the Management Development Programme.

She has designed and delivered senior leadership and general management programmes for clients around the world. At Ashridge, she heads up the people strand of the MSc in General Management which encompasses leadership, change and team-working. Her interests are predominantly in leadership, change management, influencing, coaching, and long-term sustained learning. She facilitates learning support groups and action learning sets and provides executive coaching to help improve individual performance.

Sona was born in India and is an American citizen. She has lived and worked in the US, Spain and the UK. She has over eight years of experience in the pharmaceutical industry in sales, marketing and latterly as Head of Human Resources for AstraZeneca and Human Resource Business Partner for Nortel Networks, covering Europe, and the Middle East and Asia-Pacific regions.

Sona can speak fluent Hindi and Spanish. She graduated with a BA honours degree in psychology and Spanish, and an MSc honours in organisational psychology. She is an accredited member of the British Psychological Society, holding Level A and B certificates, and has extensive experience in using psychometric tools such as Profilor, OPQ, Advanced FIRO-B,

SDI, Emotional Intelligence and Advanced Myers-Briggs Type Indicator, Strengthscope and Insights.

Educated at St Catherine's College, Oxford, and a Fellow of the Royal Society for the Arts, **Roger Delves** is Director of the Ashridge Executive Masters in Management programme and Acting Director of the Ashridge Leadership Centre. He also leads the Personal Impact MBA module and the Employability MBA module at Ashridge, works on a number of tailored programmes and is an Adjunct Professor at Hult International Business School, where in 2012 students voted him MBA Professor of the Year. His special interests are authentic leadership and the roles of integrity and ethics in management and leadership.

Roger has taught across the EU, in the Middle East, Eastern Europe, North and South America, Africa, India and Asia-Pacific. He has designed and led tailored, open and qualification programmes and is qualified in a range of psychometric instruments. His first career was in advertising, where he sat on the London board of DMB&B. He went on to be Principal Consultant in a management development consultancy and later spent six years as Programme Director at Cranfield School of Management. He has been at Ashridge since April 2008.

# Introduction

Every manager has experienced situations where they are stuck and the idea that unlocks the door eludes them. This is the book that captures the right questions, giving managers the right ideas to help discover the right direction.

Over the last decade our lives have become increasingly compressed. We are living our lives in shorter and shorter soundbites. We have gone from spending time writing letters to sending emails to sending texts to tweeting. We expect immediate responses.

In contrast, the business world is far more complex and ambiguous than ever. The need for managers to manage different points of view and opinions is greater, yet the pressure on their time is immense. Managers and leaders are too busy to wade through hundreds of books before deciding what to do. They want answers and ideas to help them move forward *now*.

At Ashridge we regularly meet managers who need to progress situations in which they feel stuck. They want good, thought-provoking ideas that will move things forward. This book has those thoughts – the ones that really matter to managers day-to-day. This means that every time you have five minutes to dip into the book, you will come away with ideas which can usefully move things forward. By providing lots of pragmatic concepts this book also helps to build the confidence of managers.

In the face of resistance or inertia many managers become tenacious, using the same tools over and over again (for example, being directive or persuasive even when that style isn't working). This book adds to your toolkit, allowing you to use a different tool when a particular approach isn't working, thereby varying your style situationally.

Of course, the choice of section titles and the selection of dilemmas is a personal one. Our choice is based on what we hear at Ashridge as we work with participants on open, tailored and qualification programmes, as we coach groups and individuals, and as we work with clients to deliver workshops which are both practical and applicable to the real working lives of teams and individuals. So even if you would have chosen different words or descriptions, we do hope these will contain useful and practical advice.

It's also possible that we may have omitted a dilemma that you are struggling with, but we hope that if you look closely enough, somewhere here will be some useful advice on which you can act which will help you to address and resolve your particular dilemma.

We owe a big thank you to all the people we have met over the last few years while we have been teaching at Ashridge, as well as to our colleagues, from whom we are constantly learning. We hope that we have listened well and that this book will be as helpful to you as our colleagues and participants have been to us.

# 1

**Challenges with individuals**

Teams consist of individuals, and the ability to manage at the individual level, to be able to meet the challenge posed by an individual, is a sure sign of an able manager. The different chapters within this section contain invaluable advice for the manager who finds just these sorts of dilemmas focused on the individual hard to deal with.

The most common management dilemmas are often those related to the needs and wants of individuals in the team. These individual behavioural dilemmas often stem from when people would rather sort out a task-related problem than deal with an issue related to how people feel about themselves or others.

The successful manager is one who is both aware of and capable of dealing with people issues. An individual's lack of motivation, confidence or competence can be a real deadweight on the rest of the team or unit. If you, as that individual's manager, can't recognise the issue or won't deal with it, then you are as responsible for the reduced performance as the individual. Once you are seen by your superiors as being unable to deal with these issues, this disinclination will be a career anchor for you – so it is worth making the effort to understand what can be done and how to set about doing it.

Equally, a modern manager cannot turn away from dilemmas which involve a lack of ethics or a lack of respect for the team's culture or way of doing things. As managers swiftly come to understand, teams and organisations get the culture they deserve, and if you understand what might be at the heart of ethical violations or issues of respect, then you will be much better able to deal with them, helping your team to optimise performance.

Every manager has to be able to have difficult conversations. Whether the conversation is around a personal turmoil which someone is working through, reflects an individual's need for attention, or is related to unacceptable or disruptive behaviour, you must either be able to initiate or to respond to these challenging exchanges. Again, not to be able to do so is to lack an essential management skill.

# Low motivation

*You've noticed that an individual who reports to you seems to have low levels of motivation. You are concerned that this is affecting their performance, and if left unmanaged, will begin to affect the rest of the team.*

## First, think:

The first thing you need to consider is whether this is someone who is new to your team or to the organisation or is an established individual who previously has been well motivated.

If it's someone new to your team:

- Does the new member seem well integrated into the team? Have the team paused and welcomed them? Has there been a proper induction into the organisation? Is the individual replacing a well-liked colleague?

- How well do you know the new team member? For example, do you know about their values? What about their personal circumstances?

- Do you know about their ambitions? Does this move represent opportunity or a step sideways? What matters more to them: work/life balance or career progression?

- Is the organisation's vision both understood and shared by this individual? Is the individual clear on the team's objectives and how they fit into the organisation's vision, and on their role in meeting team objectives?

- Is it possible there is an issue in terms of diversity?

If it's someone who has an established track record and has previously seemed motivated:

- Has something changed in their work life? Does the person have a new job role or new team members to consider? Has the individual missed out on promotion or on a particular role or project within the team?

- First you need to establish whether personal change is at the root of the lack of motivation; the next step is to scope out with the individual the impact of the change: is it likely to be short term or long term?

- Has there been recent significant culture change within the organisation – perhaps a merger or a takeover or a major new initiative around structure or process? Is there something you can do to help ease the change impact on the individual?

- Is there an opportunity to refresh their role or to give them something specific to do which you know would reignite their passion?

# Ideas for action

If it's someone who is new to your team, here are some things you can do.

### Check they aren't being excluded

Check the obvious things such as age, gender, race and cultural background. Is this person potentially feeling different or isolated due to any of these 'isms'? Don't forget, though, there are many more subtle forms of diversity. Sexual, religious or political orientation, ingrained cultural behaviours, flexi or part-time working, and working mothers can all be potential sources of disharmony within a team. In addition, people sometimes have strong working preferences and teams will have established practices. Any form of diversity can be a trigger for conflict in teams. Your role as a manager is to create a culture which values difference rather than feels threatened by it.

### Make them feel part of the team

New people can often find joining an established team daunting, as relationships are already formed. This new person may represent a significant change in the team's direction or focus and so might be seen as a threat. You need to develop a plan to integrate the person into the team. There are many books full of team-building exercise ideas. Your own HR department may also be able to offer practical support. As a general rule, the better people know each other, the better the relationships they form and the better they perform together.

## Help the team members to understand one another

If you are aware that a project is complex and long term, you should first spend time helping team members understand each other really well. Share likes and dislikes, values, attitudes and preferences so that everyone has an appreciation and understanding of one another. Particularly when new people join an established team, time spent in relationship building pays dividends.

## Appreciate differences

You also need to understand very clearly the new team member's circumstances and situation. Think about the demands on their time that their personal circumstances might make. What effect might this have on the team? You might need to decide with the individual in advance how to deal with exceptional circumstances, such as the occasional need for late working.

If the individual's attitude does not fit the team ethos then conflict will arise. The effect of this conflict may well be to lower the motivation of the individual and the team. You can help to avoid such conflict by reviewing the team charter and performance standards with the individual and gaining their commitment to it. People have legitimate pressures which require them to work in a certain way. The important thing to make sure is that the contribution they make to the team is appropriate and valued. For example, an individual whose journey time requires them to leave work at 4 p.m. may be able to stay connected by dialling in during the journey or by logging in from home in the evening.

## Make their role clear

Vision and objectives must be clearly stated and clearly understood for high performance. If you think the new individual does not clearly understand their own role and how that role contributes to the team or organisation objectives, your first step must be to ensure clarity.

All teams form a culture based on 'the way we do things around here'. So, if the team rewards extroversion and the new individual in your team is an introvert, it may make the new team member uncomfortable and affect their levels of motivation. If you suspect this might the case, you might think about asking HR to help you use one of the many team-based psychometric tools to help people in the team appreciate and value the skills and approaches that others bring to the team.

If the individual concerned is an established team member and their motivation has been getting lower, here are some things you can do.

### Find out what's changed

Have a conversation with them to discover if something has changed and if that change has caused their motivation to drop. You may need to agree an action or development plan with the person which is designed to address the problem and rebuild levels of motivation.

### Is their energy elsewhere?

You may also want to think about whether there has been some change which has affected this individual. Some people can handle significant personal change without it affecting their work, while others cannot. Many such changes are negative, but even positive changes (such as the birth of a child or marriage) can cause individuals to disengage as their emotional energy is committed elsewhere.

### Are they dealing with change poorly?

In many organisations the pace of change is increasing. People are being asked to cope with technological change, structural change and process change, often simultaneously. If they find this hard, and many do, their response may be to step back, and what you may notice is a drop in motivation. Your job is to make sure that people feel they are heard and supported. You need to make sure they feel equipped to deal with change, both emotionally and by being given the necessary new skills.

## Are they stuck in the past?

Sometimes people hanker for what they consider to be the 'good old days' and resent change and the demands the change has put on them. This is especially true if the change is imposed. Once again, you need to engage the individual in some honest conversations that result in the real reasons for the lack of motivation being acknowledged. You will need to understand the options available to you within your organisation's HR policies. You may be able to offer help such as flexi-time, short-term part-time working, or the support of the organisation's Employee Assistance Programme.

## Reawaken their commitment

Often managers forget that while they might find their own job satisfying, not everybody in their team may feel the same way about their own roles. People get bored, perhaps because they've been in the job too long or perhaps because they realise their careers are stalled. Such people regularly struggle to maintain motivation and spend their day simply going through the motions. It is important they are reminded that there are minimum standards of commitment and performance which must be maintained. If this fails, you may have a difficult decision to make: is this someone you are willing to carry or someone you need (and are able) to lose?

# Lack of confidence

*Someone who reports to you seems to have less confidence than they should in their own ability. The individual is reluctant to take on what you think are challenges which you believe are appropriate to their level and ability; the person may also be unwilling to contribute to group discussions.*

## First, think:

- Do you feel you know this person well enough to make this judgement of them? What sort of relationship do you have with them? If they are new, how much of their history do you know?
- Is this behaviour new or has the individual always lacked confidence? If it's new, has something changed? Has the team composition changed or has their job role changed? Have there been any significant changes in the organisation's structure or processes? Do you know or suspect something has changed away from work?
- Is confidence crucial to the person's current role or is it crucial for future development? Is a lack of confidence going to be a hindrance to you or to the individual?
- Finally, what kind of culture have you established within the team? Does it instil or undermine confidence?

## Ideas for action

### Confidence is in the mind

It's worth noting that women tend to explore problems at an intrinsic level first (so, a woman is more likely to question herself when things go wrong) while men examine issues extrinsically (so men will review the situation and things outside themselves to try to discover what went wrong before they question themselves). This is not to say that women lack confidence while men don't, but it does suggest that men and women might show that confidence in different ways.

### Agree with the individual that there is a problem

You should explain the specific behaviours you have noticed and the impact you believe those behaviours are having on the team. Sometimes people are unwilling to acknowledge there is a problem or are even unaware of their behaviour.

### Create a light-bulb moment

If the person is unaware that they appear to lack confidence, the simple act of bringing this to their attention can create a 'light-bulb moment'. In our teaching work at Ashridge, people often say that pertinent feedback, when sensitively given, just 'feels right' and can lead to genuine changes in behaviour. Once you have agreed that the issue needs to be addressed, you can help the individual to explore where the lack of confidence comes from: is it a lack of confidence in their competence (technical skills, organisational processes, mastery of legislation, understanding market dynamics) or is it a lack of confidence in themselves (lack of self-esteem, dealing with organisational politics, understanding interpersonal skills, navigating organisational culture)? If the lack of confidence comes from a skills deficit, you can help to identify appropriate internal or external development opportunities. Be creative in looking for development opportunities.

### Generate internal and external opportunities

External opportunities might include skills workshops but could also include secondments, action learning groups or part-time qualifications. Some industries also have useful networking or benchmarking groups; often stakeholder organisations such as clients and customers are happy to provide work-shadowing or short-term work placements. These can be used to build up an individual's skill.

Internal opportunities include partnering the individual with a knowledge expert to manage knowledge transfer, identifying a mentor who will help to fill important knowledge gaps, offering job rotation which allows the individual to focus on different aspects of the role, and providing an 'expert-buddy' to bounce questions and ideas off.

If, however, the person's lack of confidence stems from issues regarding their own self-perception, the options you can offer will be different. For example, you may wish to offer them a coach, a place on a self-development programme, or an opportunity to complete a psychometric questionnaire and receive feedback. Some people enjoy reading books to supplement learning and may find it helpful to have some recommendations made. In many cases the individual may benefit just from supportive time provided by you.

## Build the individual's confidence

Confidence is transient and fragile. Changes which might not seem significant to you can undermine the confidence of the person experiencing them. Changes in role, returning to work from maternity leave, interpersonal conflicts and changes in structure might all seem unchallenging, but each can readily undermine the confidence of an individual directly involved in or affected by them.

Think about whether you have created a high-performance culture where there is enough high support that allows high challenges to be undertaken. It is important to an individual's confidence that the culture is both positive and consistent. You must do as you say you will do. There is strong evidence that suggests people absorb and remember negative feedback far more readily than they do positive feedback. So you need to voice more specific and positive feedback and be careful about when and how you give necessary negative feedback.

## Facing up to denial

If the person is unwilling to acknowledge the problem that you perceive, there are a number of things you can consider or do.

Some individuals can deny there is a problem on the basis that they believe their preferences are to be more self-contained; this person may suggest that they have a high level of self-confidence but are by nature more quiet and withdrawn. The challenge here is to differentiate between overt confidence and quiet, self-sufficient confidence. It is important not to judge people by your own behavioural preferences.

Individuals who are confident but self-contained may be causing disharmony in the team without realising it. If in your view the individual's preferences are having a negative impact on the team, you may need to explore and agree specific ideas that you can both accept which will help the individual to impact positively on the team. For example, if the person is an introvert and requires time for reflection, you could make sure that things like agendas and documents are supplied to the team in advance. You could identify an objective third party who could (by mutual agreement) observe and offer feedback. This role should be given to someone you both respect.

# Constantly rejects feedback

*You have someone in your team who, when given feedback, always refuses to accept it and denies that it's valid. You think it's important to get this individual to see that the feedback is useful and you would like their behaviour to change because of the impact it's having on their performance and those of others in the team.*

## First, think:

There are many reasons why someone might resist feedback. The first important step is to reflect on why this individual is rejecting your feedback.

- What is their relationship with you? Do they respect you? Do you have a personal connection with them?
- Is this someone who generally has a high level of self-awareness? Or is this someone who lacks self-awareness? Do they have a history of lacking empathy or treading on people's toes? Are they more interested in getting tasks completed and their own viewpoint heard than in people and in collaborating with others?
- What about you? Are you self-aware enough to be flexible about appreciating different people's styles?
- Are you aware of what feedback they have been given in the past?
- Has anything changed within the organisation or the team? Is there any reason for the person to feel defensive or uncomfortable?
- How much feedback has this person been given? Might it feel too much or a sudden surprise? What do you know about how they like to get feedback?
- Is it possible the feedback is wrong or mistaken?

# Ideas for action

## When the issue is a lack of awareness

There are lots of behaviours which tell you if people aren't good at receiving feedback. Poor listening skills, apparent arrogance, defensiveness and a general lack of empathy are some of them. All of these may be due to the individual's relative lack of self-awareness.

## Feedback is about and for the receiver

A key challenge about feedback is that it can often be as much about the giver as about the receiver. We all tend to give feedback from our perspective on life, based on our value systems and our experiences. It's important to be aware of how you like to do things and then to be sure you are not criticising others simply because they like to do things in a different way. Receiving feedback is a highly individual thing. Some of us love it and want it by the bucketload, while others prefer their feedback in very small doses and only from people they know very well and for whom they have lots of respect.

## Pushing back may be appropriate

Bear in mind that if this feedback contradicts previous feedback others have provided, the individual may rightfully push back. However, if, in your view, this person lacks self-awareness then part of your responsibility as a manager is to help them develop a better understanding of themselves. You might suggest that they complete a psychometric questionnaire with professional feedback or as part of a development programme.

## Context is key to giving feedback appropriately

Think about the context of your organisation: in some companies, feedback is a prevalent part of the culture while elsewhere it is given once a year (if that) during performance reviews. Remember, too, that people and organisations differ in formality; some are more formal and conservative while others are much less structured and more open. Some people and organisations are more circumspect, some are more direct. Bearing all of that in mind before giving feedback will improve the quality of your feedback and also the likelihood that it will be well received. Feedback must be appropriate both to the recipient and to the culture.

## Flex your style for best results

Your style for giving feedback will need to vary keeping in mind all of the above but also the nature of the feedback being given. You may choose to be informal and impromptu (over lunch or even outside the workplace) when giving someone feedback that is less critical in nature, whereas you may find a more formal environment better suited to feedback which is particularly critical.

To minimise the chances of your feedback being rejected, remember BOOST: Balanced, Observed, Objective, Specific, Timely. Feedback should be a balance of praise and constructive criticism. Don't pass on third-party comments as feedback. This not only leaves you in a vulnerable situation (what if the recipient disputes what you have said or your information proves to be inaccurate?) but also it isn't fair on the other person (because the feedback is unsubstantiated). Feedback is a lot more likely to be accepted if it is specific and observed. Giving someone feedback weeks after the event will not serve you or them very well; the impact and the relevance are long gone. This is often difficult for managers with very busy diaries who must ensure they make time for regular feedback with their reports. Done well, it's a powerful tool to contribute to high performance and a positive culture.

Particularly when giving feedback, it helps the giver and the receiver if there is some structure to the feedback provided. Here are some useful structures which you could adapt for your situation and for the person to whom you are giving feedback. You can expand on these examples as you plan your feedback session.

- **Stop, Start, Continue** – to address the issue, what should they stop doing, start doing and continue to do? Make sure you finish with the positive behaviours they should maintain.

- **BOFF: Behaviour, Outcome, Feelings, Future** – summarise the unhelpful behaviour and its outcome or impact on the team. Follow this up with how it's making you feel and what you'd like to see changed in the future.

- **EEC: Example, Effect, Change** – give a specific example of unhelpful behaviour; explain the effect the behaviour has had and suggest a change which will remove the problem.

## Asking can be as effective as telling

If you think someone is likely to resist feedback, it's often better to start with a question rather than a statement. Sometimes asking questions is a good way of opening the door to a good exchange of views. It is especially useful when the individual is withdrawn or defensive and finds interpersonal communication too challenging. A good technique is to engage with a 'questioning funnel'. Start with open questions to generate a flow of information. Then ask probing questions to gain clarity. Finally, use closed questions to agree an outcome.

Feedback is vital in a high-performing team – the main thing is to build a team culture where constant feedback is the norm rather than the exception. Encouraging regular, open conversations with your team members will help to build a culture where people feel able to discuss their views and concerns without being defensive. That in turn will help the team make better-quality decisions and encourage the team to buy in to decisions that are made.

# Lack of competence

*You notice someone in your team lacks the job-based competence that you would expect them to have. You can't trust them to deliver to the standard required of their position.*

## First, think:

A key consideration here is whether this is someone who is new to your team or to the organisation or whether it is an established individual who previously has been competent. Alternatively, it may be that you're new to the team and you find yourself unhappy with the performance of someone you've been told is competent.

If it's someone new to your team, you may want to reflect on the following points:

- Do you support new joiners appropriately to help them contribute quickly?
- Is their competency shortfall unexpected? Was their competency discussed and/or evaluated during the selection process?
- How quickly can you address the shortfall? Is skills training available?

If it's someone who has an established track record within your team and has previously been competent, you may want to consider some of these points:

- Has anything changed within their job role? Are they now required to do different things or work with different people as a result of changes imposed on them (by you or by the organisation)?
- Has anything changed within their personal life? Has anything altered to affect their attitude towards the organisation or their team?

If you're new to the team and you find yourself managing someone you have been told is competent but you find not to be, you may want to consider:

- How do they feel about your appointment?
- How do they feel about their future prospects?
- How do your standards compare to the previous manager's?
- Do you know about the history of this individual within the organisation?

# Ideas for action

## New people need special care

If it's someone who is new to your team who appears to lack competence, here are some things you can do.

Joining a new team or organisation may require a few weeks or even months of settling in. As someone comes to grips with the role, the culture, the nature of the business and the stakeholders involved, it may be that there is a short-term dip in performance while they acclimatise to their new role. It's easy to forget how it feels to be new: there is a huge volume of information for new joiners to take on board.

There should be a structured induction plan which covers the competencies required. If appropriate, your induction plan could allow for shadowing opportunities with a competent colleague and, if the role requires interface with other departments, opportunities to sit in those departments in order to understand their role and priorities.

If you weren't part of the selection process, you need to find out everything you can about the individual's performance during that interview or assessment. What were the key strengths and were any gaps identified? As soon as you're aware of gaps you need an action plan to close them. This might include offering in-company skills development, external courses, mentoring or a buddy-system. However, if it's a serious competency shortfall, you may want to familiarise yourself with their contractual probationary period.

## But established team members need *different* special care

If it's an established team member and their competence has declined, here are some things you can do.

Regardless of changes in professional or private circumstances, individuals must be able to maintain a level of professional competence. While organisational or personal changes can lead to acceptable short-term changes in behaviour, as a manager you can't allow a drop in competence. You can be flexible about short-term changes in behaviour; however, you will need to act swiftly to correct and redirect deterioration in performance.

## Watch for and notice attitude shifts

It takes a while for a change in attitude to manifest itself in a drop in performance. When you observe a performance drop you should always explore the possibility that the individual's attitude towards you, their job role or the organisation has changed. You won't improve their performance until you address their change in attitude.

## When it's you who's new, different things can happen

If it's you who is new to the team and by your standards someone is under-performing, consider the following. If this person was interested in getting your job, they may be angry or frustrated at your appointment. Consciously or unconsciously, they may be hampering your success. You do need to sit down and call them on it. However they feel about your appointment, you cannot allow it to affect their performance.

If your appointment affects their perception about their future prospects, the same thing applies. You can, and should, address their concerns with them. You should point out that future progress will be performance related. In the majority of organisations career prospects are directly linked to job performance. So, however they feel, they must perform to the required standard. It is in their interests as well as yours.

## Don't demand inappropriate or unreasonable standards

Think about your own ambitions and your expectations of yourself and others. There is a link between the standards you set yourself and those you demand of others. Is the job-based competence standard you are setting too high? Even if, on reflection, there is room for improvement in this individual's performance, you need to consider whether you have set a reasonable timeframe within which the improvement needs to happen.

You need to acknowledge the implicit or explicit history of performance the individual has with the organisation. If they have generally been given positive performance reviews, you should bear this in mind when you decide how to frame the feedback you want to offer.

## Help people realise their potential

Part of your responsibility as a manager is to help every individual realise their potential. Your role is to develop the capabilities of the people you manage. You have an equal responsibility to maintain performance standards at an appropriate level. A team is only as strong as its weakest link. This, however, is a difficult balancing act to maintain. Your organisation's HR function can help you to develop individuals; it can also help you to remove people who do not and cannot reach the required standard. Sometimes companies outgrow people: the same person who was a star performer when the company was smaller can become ineffective when the company grows larger. A final point to remember: when you do shut a door for an individual, asking them to leave the organisation, you should be able to do it softly.

# Unethical behaviour

*Someone who reports to you is behaving in a way that you consider to be professionally unethical. You are concerned about both what the individual is doing and the risk to the team's reputation.*

## First, think:

There are lots of different definitions of ethics and ethical behaviour. For the purposes of this book we have defined ethics as 'the rules that govern our behaviour'. We might equally use terms such as 'values' or 'principles' to capture this same idea. The important thing is to focus on the behaviour in the situation at hand:

- Is it a clear and obvious violation of the rules? Is it an obvious violation of your own or the organisation's values? Is it an example of conflicting country cultural norms? Is what you see as a violation acceptable within that individual's national culture?

- Is it a result of a compelling business imperative? Might the individual's justification for that behaviour be that it is in the best interest of the business?

- Are you sure your concern is about the behaviour rather than your reaction to the individual? How honest are you being with yourself?

- Is your reaction to the behaviour likely to be shared by the majority of people in the organisation? Is it likely to be shared by people outside the organisation?

- Are you confident that you know the company and the people within it well enough to be sure that what you see as a violation will be seen as such by others?

- Are you sure you understand and are interpreting correctly the behaviour that you see? Do you have all the facts you need?
- Do you understand and are you prepared to accept the consequences of challenging this behaviour?

# Ideas for action

## Rule breaking versus values violation

The first thing you must think about is whether this is a behaviour which breaks organisational rules or whether it is behaviour which offends your values (bear in mind it could do both).

Examples of rule-breaking behaviour (which might also offend values):

- Money laundering
- Expenses falsification
- Using company time for personal tasks
- Bribing customers
- Accepting gifts and hospitality

Examples of behaviours that offend values (which might also break rules):

- Coercion or bullying
- Dishonesty
- Personal use of office equipment
- Discrimination, sexism, ageism
- Profanity

## Culture creates and manages behaviours

Every company and every country has different cultural norms. These govern and regulate our daily behaviour. Even the same company, when it operates in many different countries, will find that different cultural norms exist in each of those different countries. There are challenges when the cultural norms in a country clash with the values or the rules of the individual or the organisation working in that country. For example, in some parts of the world bribery is acceptable and in others it is unacceptable.

## Business imperatives can challenge rules or values

Another challenge is when the business imperative leads to behaviours that offend either rules or values. For example, a large contract might be endangered unless it is entirely staffed by male executives.

It is really important to have clarity about exactly what is offending you and why. This is a complex and ambiguous area in which many different views are held by all the various stakeholders who are involved. It is very important when addressing ethical dilemmas to arrive at a solution which seems both good and just to you. This is easier to do if both you and the organisation are aligned and are clear about what is and is not allowable and what the penalty is for violation.

If you are not aligned with the organisation's views, the risk is that you appear to be a troublemaker and meddling unnecessarily. Alternatively, if you have no firmly developed views of your own around what is and isn't right, then the risks are that you:

- ignore the situation but therefore risk appearing to collude or being seen to be weak;
- address the part of the situation you feel 'safest' to deal with confidently;
- address the situation but do it badly or inappropriately;
- start to take action but withdraw when things get difficult or complex.

The dominant need is to create a clear and complete understanding of the facts. Without this, any action you take is likely to be grounded in misconception. It is always a good idea to bounce your views off a colleague or a friend whose opinion you respect. By their nature these issues are tricky ones. We all take comfort from knowing that our intended course of action meets with the approval of someone we respect.

## Self-interest is usually central to unethical behaviour

When you're thinking about an individual's behaviour that concerns you, it's worth looking through the lens of that person's self-interest. Often this will help you to understand why they are behaving as they are; this will in turn help you to decide how to address it. If the infringement is minor you will probably want to address it informally. Even so, remember that the first time you raise the issue is when you have the best chance of getting an honest, raw response. In any subsequent meetings you risk coming up against a more polished and considered defence.

If the infringement is more serious, once you are clear about the facts you should seek advice. At a minimum you need to speak with both a senior in-company HR professional and a mentor whose advice you respect. The first critical thing to establish is whether either of these two sources believes that the behaviour that is concerning you is in breach of the organisation's rules or guidelines. Next you need to make sure that both of these sources of advice can and will support you if you take this matter further. Pursuing ethical violations is demanding; you can't underestimate the amount of practical and emotional support you will need.

Another possibility is that the unacceptable behaviour is something that violates your sense of integrity but not the company's. In these cases you have a far more difficult decision to make: do you apply your sense of what is right and wrong, or the organisation's sense?

## Whistle-blowing can be the lonely option

There are well-documented cases of whistle-blowers in the press. If you decide to blow the whistle on an individual or an organisation, you should be prepared for a long and difficult journey which may well not end in success. This is not to say that you should not take action in the face of ethical violations; you should simply be prepared for the storm.

There is likely to be an impact on the team when these sorts of issues come to light. You will need to spend time with the team to repair any damage done to the team's culture. You may also need to make yourself even more available than usual for conversations with affected team members.

# Unobserved but reported disrespectful behaviour

*You have a team member who appears to respect you; however, others tell you this individual acts disrespectfully towards you when you aren't there. The behaviour is affecting individuals and the team as a whole. This is particularly tricky because the behaviour isn't directly observed but rather has been reported to you via third parties.*

## First, think:

- Does this represent a change in this individual's behaviour? If so, can you link the change to any other particular events or circumstances?
- Is the disrespect restricted to you alone? Is it possible there is a valid reason for this disrespect, perhaps to do with the way you lead or your own personal integrity? Do you set an appropriate example in this area yourself? Are you known to say one thing to someone's face and another behind their back?
- What about the culture that you have set in your team? Is it really one of honesty, transparency and authenticity?
- Can you trust the feedback that has been given to you? Has the same feedback been corroborated by more than one person?
- Is there a bigger picture, perhaps to do with office politics, organisational change or personal ambition?
- What is the downside to addressing this? To not addressing it?

# Ideas for action

## Understand what is driving the behaviour

Disrespectful behaviour is often a symptom of something else. So, dealing with the disrespectful behaviour may not actually address the underlying problem. As with so many other aspects of management, it is vital that you really know your staff well; you should be able to feel, almost intuitively, the nuances in your team. Another challenge is that disrespectful behaviour comes in many forms. For example, an individual may:

- talk disparagingly about you behind your back;
- take credit for your ideas or work;
- undermine your decisions;
- question your judgement;
- agree a course of action and then drag their feet;
- exceed their authority with clients, customers or colleagues.

## Don't model the wrong behaviour

Is it possible that you are unconsciously sending a message to your team that it's OK to say one thing to someone's face and another thing behind their back? Is it even possible that the disrespectful remarks are true? Leaders often forget how carefully they are observed: generally speaking, anything you are seen to do is assumed to be acceptable behaviour within the team. There is a metaphor of the leader as a lighthouse: the light shines widely and over a long distance and the fog horn can be heard for many miles around. The behaviour modelled by leaders is amplified.

If, after a cold, hard look at your own behaviour, you decide either that this individual is simply mirroring your behaviour or that there is some truth in the reported comments, then you need to focus on changing yourself before challenging the individual. Only if this does not change the individual's behaviour would you need to address the problem more directly.

## Be sure before you take action

A second challenge is the reliability of the feedback given to you. A good principle regarding feedback is that it should be given by the observer to the observed. Giving feedback to someone based on another person's observation can cause conflict within the relationship between those two individuals. Also, it is easy for someone to rebut feedback when the provider hasn't actually seen the behaviour. It becomes difficult for the feedback provider to stand by the feedback in the face of denial if they have not witnessed for themselves the behaviour on which they are giving feedback.

A good course of action is always to try to observe the behaviour for yourself. For example, if you are told that someone has become argumentative in front of clients, before addressing the issue with the individual make a point of attending a few client meetings with the individual. Try to see for yourself the behaviour which is concerning others.

If you find yourself faced with a situation where this is not possible (for example, if someone is said to be talking about you behind your back) then the first thing you need to decide is how much trust you place in the feedback you are getting. Generally speaking, the more people giving you the same feedback and the more you trust the people who are giving you feedback, the more you can be sure there is a real issue.

In this type of situation, you might consider one of two options. You could ask one or two of the feedback providers to attend a meeting with you and the individual. This won't be an easy meeting and it will call heavily on your good facilitation skills so that no one feels unfairly exposed. Alternatively you could ask the feedback providers if they are happy to be named in a meeting you would have with the individual concerned. In this case you would need good-quality detail, ideally from more than one observer, to discuss in the meeting.

Disrespectful behaviour must always be addressed. If you don't do so, you are not only encouraging others to act the same way but also allowing poison to spread in your team.

## Deal with the cause, not just the effect

It is vital that you address the behaviour itself *and* unearth the reasons behind the behaviour. Disrespectful behaviour is often a symptom of an underlying cause. Before the meeting you might think about what underlying causes might exist. Is there individual or organisational change in the air?

New team members (especially experienced individuals) often find it difficult not to compare their current team and team leader with past teams and past team leaders. People can come into teams with a sense of regret and loss which causes them to criticise you or the team. It might be important for them for you to acknowledge this sense of loss so they can move on.

Perhaps the culture this individual has left behind really is better than the culture you have set for your team. This might be a great incentive for you to re-evaluate and change your team's culture. Equally, the individual may have come from a culture where it was the norm to behave in this way. In this case you may need to emphasise the different culture that exists within the team they have joined. Thinking about and understanding potential underlying causes will help you to decide how best to help them change their behaviour.

## Personal or political agendas can drive disrespectful behaviour

Disrespect can be politically motivated. Does the individual have anything to gain by undermining you and your position? One of the quickest ways to fragment a team is for self-directed political activity to become widespread. It is important that you address this issue directly and firmly with the individual.

Unaddressed disrespectful behaviour from one individual simply gives permission for everyone else in the team to be disrespectful. This negative behaviour is infectious and swiftly becomes rife.

If the disrespect is restricted to you alone then you need to establish whether it's disrespect or dislike that you're facing. It is quite possible to work in a successful team with someone who doesn't like you; it is far harder to do so with someone who doesn't respect you. Think about a successful soccer team: would you pass to someone you don't like? The answer is probably yes. Would you pass to someone whose ability you don't respect? The answer is probably no.

## Demand professionalism, seek respect

If you find someone in your team genuinely doesn't respect you, there is a minimum requirement of them that they behave professionally. You might want to explore why they don't respect you and what you can do about that, but the minimum requirement must be demanded of them. It is not professional to be openly disrespectful about your team leader.

If, despite your best endeavours, the individual cannot and will not respect you or your position, that may be grounds for dismissal in many organisations. At a minimum you will want to involve HR and take steps to remove this individual from your team.

# High performers who are high maintenance

*You have a team member who is very good at what they do but demands a lot of attention. This individual may dominate meetings, demand a lot of one-on-one time, have pet projects or opinions which they frequently voice, or in some other way require a great deal of your time.*

## First, think:

- The first thing to consider is what impact this behaviour is having on you. What about the team? Does it extend to internal or external stakeholders? Where and how do allowances have to be made? Is the individual worth the extra time?
- Do you think you have any chance of changing these high-maintenance behaviours? How might the individual react if you challenge these behaviours?
- Is it acceptable for someone in your team to be high maintenance in this way? Are you doing anything that makes this individual believe these behaviours are acceptable?
- What is the organisational culture? Does the organisation value results enough to accept high-maintenance individuals who deliver?
- Do other team members feel this individual gets special treatment?
- Different people have different tolerances for different behaviours: do you know where your lines are drawn?

# Ideas for action

## High-maintenance behaviour comes in many forms

For example, an individual may:

- demand a lot of attention and one-on-one time;
- ignore 'the way we do things around here' and/or values;
- make unilateral decisions;
- pick and choose how and when they engage with the team;
- selectively choose the rules they will observe;
- need a lot of emotional support;
- be overly stubborn and argumentative.

## What is the effort needed from you? What is the effect on the team?

Before you decide whether you're going to take action, you need to think about three things. First, is this high-performing individual going to be worth the effort you will have to make? Your commitment is not just one of time and energy: are you willing to take the risk that your actions might cause the individual to quit the team or that the individual's unwillingness to change may cause you to require them to leave?

Secondly, you have to think about how this individual is affecting others in the team and the team's culture. If you choose not to address these behaviours, you must accept that the signal you are giving to the team is that results far outweigh the importance of team values.

Finally, will you have support for any action from key stakeholders such as senior management, given that the individual delivers results?

Your views and decisions on all of these points will impact the actions you will take.

## Be precise, honest and prepared

If you decide to take action, the first thing to do is to establish the exact nature of their high-maintenance behaviour and which aspects you want to challenge. Because this is a difficult area to tackle, you must be sure that their behaviours go beyond the merely irritating and are indeed unacceptable. Next you need to decide how you are going to broach the subject with the individual. Be aware that many high-maintenance individuals may be defensive when they are challenged about their behaviours.

You must reflect on your own actions to date. Have you tacitly given approval for these behaviours? Even by ignoring high-maintenance behaviour you are implicitly supporting it. The longer you have been accepting the behaviour, the harder it will be to address it.

You have to be very well prepared, give lots of specific examples, and be willing to be assertive. Many high-maintenance individuals don't realise the effect their behaviours have on others in the team. They focus on the results they achieve and therefore believe that their behaviours are a large part of their success. You have to acknowledge their success but get them to realise that their high-maintenance behaviours limit their success rather than maximise it, not least because of the effect of their behaviours on others in the team.

## Barrier for their future ambition

An issue for high-maintenance individuals which they may not realise is that their behaviours quickly become a barrier to career progression. Management rarely want to promote high-maintenance individuals beyond their operational role. There is research about high performers whose careers plateau or derail not because of the results they achieve but because of their individualistic, self-orientated behaviours. Leadership and management are about listening to others and getting things done through others, rather than pursuing individual success. This is a difficult message for such people to hear, but if they are ambitious for a leadership or management role, it may be the strongest lever you can use.

## Challenging the behaviour

In your management role, individuals like this present a big challenge because they really do deliver results. Having decided it's important to take action, the authentic manager will find a way to address this problem. The line of least resistance is an option often selected by the less confident manager. This is only a good option if you believe you will not have support if you address the problem.

You need to assess whether this behaviour is being demonstrated as a way of seeking attention because of insecurity or due to arrogance. If you believe this person has low self-esteem, you need to set about trying to build their confidence. However, if there is arrogance at play you must not only address the behaviour but also be seen by others to be doing so. The team needs to know you have noticed the inappropriate behaviour and are taking steps to address it.

Changing the behaviour of these people takes time, so you must at the same time address the impact the individual has on the team. This impact can be very divisive. The normal rule says 'praise in public, criticise in private'; however, in this situation where you are reacting to an issue which has already impacted on members of the team, if you do not acknowledge that the issue exists it becomes 'an elephant in the room' which can even further damage the team morale.

Even in these circumstances, though, you should limit yourself to acknowledging the problem and explaining that you are addressing it. You shouldn't divulge specifics of the conversations you have had with the individual. However you do it, you must convince the individual that in future there will be consequences attached to their high-maintenance behaviour.

The actions you can impose range from, for example, stopping their interruptions during meetings to insisting they follow established team rules. You have to find a sanction which is compelling enough to cause the individual to change their unacceptable behaviour. In the end, the ultimate sanction of dismissal from the team or organisation may have to be at least considered.

# Personal turmoil

*You have a team member who is going through significant personal turmoil, to the point where it is adversely affecting their professional performance. The individual appears distracted and disengaged. This in turn is affecting the team's ability to act as a high-performing unit.*

## First, think:

- How well do you know this person? How long have they been in your team?
- How open is this person to you and to others in the team about their personal issues? Is this personal turmoil work-based or based outside work? How long has this been going on? Is there an end in sight?
- Is the cause of the turmoil something that can be changed or something that cannot be changed? Does this individual need your protection, your support, your advice or none of these things?
- Have they asked for help from you? Do you feel personally able to get involved? Are they seeking help from outside the organisation? Do you have to get HR involved?
- What compromises (if any) have you had to make so far? What impact has this had on you or the team? Is there a deterioration in performance? What about their relationships within the team? How is this affecting the rest of the team?
- Do you have an option to do nothing?

# Ideas for action

## Get to know the individual properly

If you can't answer a lot of these questions, then before you try to address the effects of the turmoil you probably need to know more about the person, their turmoil and the ramifications for the team.

If you have any concerns that the root of this turmoil is clinical or medical, you must refer the individual to the appropriate support system within the organisation. Don't try to engage with something beyond your competence. Sometimes well-intentioned team leaders, in trying to help a valued team member, can inadvertently do more harm than good.

## Performance affecting turmoil must be addressed

What has brought this issue to your attention? Sit down informally and explain to the individual what you have observed. You may find that they are willing to open up to you on a confidential basis about what is happening and what help they need from you.

If you have seen an impact on performance (individual or team) then you must take action. However difficult it is, you must have an open conversation with the individual which acknowledges that there is a performance aspect which must be addressed. The outcome needs to ensure that the turmoil will not continue to affect performance to the point where the team or the business suffers. You may be able to cut them some slack in some areas (for example, by allowing more work from home or flexible working hours for a period of time) while emphasising areas in which performance shortfall can't be allowed.

## Help individuals manage turmoil

If there is no performance impact but you feel this person is becoming disengaged, you have a decision to make. You can choose to become involved early or you can choose to wait until there is an impact on performance. The choice you make is likely to be informed by the specific circumstances and your relationship with the individual.

If you are being asked for help by the individual, are you properly equipped? Willing to do what is asked? Able to do so? For example, if the cause of the turmoil is something deeply personal like the end of a relationship with a colleague, you might not feel equipped to help. Equally, you may not feel it is part of your professional responsibility and therefore you may be unwilling to help. However, if the cause is, for example, some form of discrimination which offends company values, then you will have no option but to act.

Perhaps you are being asked for advice in an area in which you are not competent (for example, a legal matter regarding divorce proceedings). Here you may not feel able to help even if you are willing. In each case you need to be very clear with the individual and explain why you are doing what you are doing.

## Get involved for the right reasons

If you haven't been asked for help but feel you must get involved, make sure you're getting involved because it's right for the individual rather than just for your own reasons. People have a right to keep things private; as a manager your right is to address the effects on performance.

Saying that, good managers often feel personally committed to individuals within their teams. The more you have invested time and energy in getting to know your team members as individuals, the more likely they are to be open with you about their personal circumstances. It's often better to wait for individuals to approach you about personal challenges – just make sure that you are often available for informal conversations.

## Long-term and short-term turmoil are different

If the cause of the turmoil is something that is likely to go on for a long time, such as a deteriorating illness, you need to develop an action plan with the individual. You may need to involve HR in these instances, depending on your organisation's policies.

If the turmoil is short-term with an end in sight (for example, moving house) then you may well be able to make specific, time-bound compromises which address the effects of the challenges being faced.

As the team manager, and regardless of whether the individual is acknowledging that there is a degree of personal turmoil, you may want to encourage other team members to make some allowances for that individual – one of which may be not to ask about or acknowledge the turmoil.

## Positive cultures most help those in turmoil

These kinds of situations arise in every team and are a good test of the team's culture. Can the team continue to be supportive and high-performing despite one individual's difficult personal circumstances? The best teams can. Tests such as these help you as the manager to explore appropriate levels of flexibility within the team's culture.

# Difficult and delicate conversations

*Managers today look after increasingly diverse teams. Many managers find it very challenging to tackle tricky conversations such as those concerning inappropriate office relationships, interpersonal conflict, aspects of personal hygiene or appearance, challenges arising from racial or religious diversity, and issues related to alcohol, drugs or smoking, etc. However, you should be aware that an unwillingness to take on these sorts of conversations is likely to hold back your own career progression.*

## First, think:

- Are you better at addressing performance issues relating to an individual's task than at addressing personal or interpersonal issues?
- What guidance (if any) is provided by your organisation's HR policies to help manage the issue you need to address?
- What impact is the issue having on the team and other stakeholders?
- What are the reactions you might encounter that worry you?
- How did this issue come to your attention? Is it something you noticed yourself, or has it been brought to your attention by someone else?
- Are you comfortable with diversity yourself?

# Ideas for action

## Conversations of this type are called difficult and delicate for a reason!

It is often easier to deal with the pragmatic, task-orientated aspects of management while avoiding these more sensitive areas. However, successful managers have to be adept at instigating conversations which they know will not be well received. The decision is not *whether* you have the conversation; it is *how* to have the conversation.

## Be clear whether this is a performance-related issue or something more personal

- Examples of a difficult conversation around personal issues might be challenging an individual about a relationship with a client which is affecting team harmony, discussing a team member's lunchtime drinking habits, questioning an individual's too-revealing outfit, or addressing inappropriate office banter around homosexuality or religion.

- Examples of performance-related issues where you will need to have a difficult or delicate conversation might be significant interpersonal conflict which is affecting the wider team's performance, unwillingness to stay updated professionally, refusal to work beyond contractual obligation, or consistent unpunctuality.

## Clarity is absolutely vital

The more difficult or delicate the conversation, the more important it is to be absolutely clear about your criticism and about the action that you need the other person to take. There can be no ambiguity or opportunity for misinterpretation. It's often useful to engage with a trusted advisor. First you should check out the legitimacy of the criticism you intend to offer. Does your advisor agree that this conversation must be had? If so, take the opportunity to rehearse the actual conversation you intend to have.

If there is an HR policy which covers the issue you are trying to address, this will make your conversation easier. Be sure you know exactly what the policy is and how it applies to the issue you are facing. The policy can give structure and content to your conversation.

If the difficult conversation is based on someone else reporting a potential issue to you, then it's imperative that you make sure there is substance to the issue. Be clear that the report is accurate and not malicious before you take any action.

## Be prepared

You can't enter a conversation such as this expecting to make it up as you go along. There will be too much pressure on you, especially if you are out of your comfort zone. This really is a case of 'failing to prepare is preparing to fail'.

Get the simple things right: don't have this type of conversation in front of others, or when either of you is in a hurry, or when other things are pressing on you, or if you are already angry or impatient with the individual.

Don't create a shopping list of criticisms relating to a particular individual and then go through the list one by one. Not only does this dilute your message but it makes you appear to be a 'strict parent'.

## Use open cultures to foster honest conversations

As a broad rule of thumb, it is good to create a culture in which everyone has frequent open and honest conversations about what is and what isn't going well as a team and individually. The more frequent these conversations are the better people become at having them; this in turn means that more and more difficult subjects can be openly discussed. It also means that each individual conversation appears to be less freighted with importance, and individuals aren't automatically anxious when you instigate a conversation.

## Learn from the past

Closely examine what has gone well in difficult conversations you have had in the past. Use this as the basis for your own personal style around such conversations in the future. It is really important to be authentically yourself in these conversations; if you are not, people will immediately realise that you are behaving differently and raise barriers.

## Understand the other person ... and yourself

Vital to the success of these conversations is your ability to understand the person you will be addressing and to anticipate how that person may react to what is being said. You must consider very carefully what you know or need to know about this individual, so that before the conversation starts you have the clearest possible picture.

## Don't let your values eclipse those of the organisation

Often these types of delicate issues are highly personal. You must balance an individual's right to privacy with your need to establish whether a concern genuinely exists and the situation needs to be addressed. It is quite possible for someone to offend against your subjective personal values without being in breach of the organisation's rules (both formal and informal). For example, you might disapprove of individuals forming a close, personal relationship, but it may not be something disallowed by the organisation.

# Delegation and letting go

*Promotion to manager is often dependent on personal perfor-mance. Often managers are concerned that those things that they were rewarded for are now things they need to let go. It's difficult but necessary to let go of the things that made your reputation and to embrace the things that will further your reputation. Delegation, on the other hand, is the important skill of knowing what parts of your job you can, and should, give to others to help them grow and develop. You will find there may be barriers to doing this.*

## First, think:

- Why were you promoted? To carry on doing the things you were doing but at a higher level, or to do different things? What are your particular skills – the things for which you are valued and that make you stand out?
- Do you know what is expected of your team? How can you help them to grow and develop so that they can exceed these expectations?
- How well do you understand what delegation is and how to delegate successfully and sensibly?
- What is your historical record around delegation? Have you delegated well, wisely and successfully? If not, what barriers have you encountered? How will you remove these barriers in the future?
- How well do you think you understand the principles and practice of succession management? Have you benefited in the past from someone else's careful succession planning?

# Ideas for action

## Delegation wins you time

A common concern among managers is that they don't have enough time to do their jobs as well as they would want. It doesn't seem to matter how hard or how long they work, there never seems to be enough time; the things that don't get done are often those things that are important but not yet urgent. The manager ends up being very task orientated. Delegation gives managers more time. There are some clear barriers to delegation which you need to acknowledge and overcome: some are organisational but the bulk are personal barriers.

## Objectively assess what you do

Take a step back and put together a review of your work-based activities for a typical week. This will allow you to evaluate objectively how you spend your time. You will also be able to see and recognise those tasks which you particularly enjoy doing. What you have to do is be very firm with yourself and stop doing those tasks which are no longer appropriate to your new role, however much you enjoy doing them. Letting go of some parts of your previous role can be difficult, whether because those were the tasks you were rewarded for doing well in the past or that you particularly enjoyed, or because you feel nobody can do them to your high standards, or because this means losing your ability to keep your ear to the ground.

## Clearly understand what you should be doing

If you don't have a clear job description, it's important to create one. You can do this by discussing the role with your boss, your mentor and any other stakeholders you think appropriate. Without a clear job description it's almost impossible to decide how you should be spending your time. When you're promoted, generally you are expected to take on new responsibilities and challenges. Once you know what people expect of you and how you will be measured, think about how you will need to change what you do and how you do it. Think about who can help you embrace the role into which you have been promoted.

## Delegate for the benefit of others as well as yourself

An important part of delegation is to delegate away things which allow other people in your team to develop their skills while at the same time freeing you up for important but not necessarily urgent aspects of your job (for example, strategic thinking). From the review sheet you have created which captures how you spend your time, compile the following lists: a list of things you must continue to do yourself; a list of things you can delegate to your team straight away; and finally, a list of things you should be able to delegate in 6 to 12 months' time as team members develop under your guidance. Now write down a list of the people in your team, noting their current skills and your sense of their future potential. Map these onto the tasks you can delegate right now and those you hope to delegate in the future. This should give you a clear picture of what can be delegated to whom and when.

Writing a review sheet of your work-based activities and a separate list of the skills and areas for development of the individuals in your team will help you to be objective about what you delegate and to whom. It's important that you don't just give away the mundane or unpleasant aspects of your own job. You should delegate to grow the skills of the individual to whom you are delegating and not to benefit yourself.

## Delegation is incremental and not absolute

Remember that delegation does not necessarily require you to hand over every aspect of a task to somebody else. There are levels of delegation. You may find someone in your team who requires your direction and needs more guidance. This may be because they are new to their role or project or to the organisation. You may also have team members who would benefit from being delegated tasks which you would then coach them through. These individuals require the sort of coaching support that is offered by open questions and your careful listening. The next level of delegation is that of support, where you are available to help and where no decision is taken without your agreement but your team member has more freedom and more responsibility. The final level of delegation is one reserved for team members in whom you have complete trust and who, in your opinion, are able to complete what needs to be done to the required standard without supervision.

In our experience most of the barriers to delegation are personal. It's your unwillingness to stop doing what you like doing or your concern that delegation will make you less visible which prevents you delegating as much or as frequently as you could. Rather than thinking about why you should *not* delegate, focus instead on why you *should* delegate. Delegation creates the time for you to spend on aspects of the job where you add most value, and this is how you will build your own reputation and career.

## Delegation helps you to assess and develop your team and the people within it

There are significant additional advantages to knowing the strengths and development areas of the individuals in your team. For example, this knowledge is an important step on the path to succession planning. Delegation itself contributes to succession planning because it allows you to evaluate progress and the potential of individuals in the workplace.

# Dominant people

*An important aspect of a team that functions well is that everyone's voice is able to be heard and different views are respected. Dominant people can endanger this balance, making it more difficult for the quieter or more reticent colleagues to make their contribution. Dominant behaviour is often unconscious, which means that if it is not challenged and checked it will continue unabated.*

## First, think:

- Do you feel you understand what represents dominant behaviour, how to recognise it and what effect it may have on a team or group?
- How happy are you with the culture within the team? Do you feel everyone is treated and heard equally? If not, how do you really feel about this imbalance?
- Is dominant behaviour challenged or checked within the team? If so, who does so? What happens if this behaviour is challenged?
- Who suffers because of the dominant person or people? What does the team lose as a result of this person or these people suffering?
- Do you do or say anything to cause dominant people to think their behaviour is actually admired and rewarded? Are you a dominant individual yourself or do you openly or covertly admire dominant behaviour? Does the organisation's culture reward dominant behaviour?
- What do you think the individual expects or hopes to gain by trying to dominate? What can you do to draw the individual's attention to their own behaviour?

# Ideas for action

### It's about the individuals within the team

As a manager you need to be aware not only of the culture that exists within the team but also of individual preferences and styles; you also need to understand clearly the impact of your own behaviours. Important to the development of the team's culture is your personal style and preference as the team leader. For example, you might perceive interruptions during a team meeting as positive and adding to a 'brainstorming culture', whereas another member of the team might view the same activity negatively, feeling oppressed or disrespected. You have to be sure that you don't reward behaviours that inadvertently exclude team members or make it hard for them to join in.

### Dominant behaviour always creates victims

Sometimes you will notice who these victims are and sometimes they may come to you and complain about what is happening to them. You have a responsibility to the people in your team, so you will need to address this issue. If you're responding to an individual's complaint and you haven't noticed any inappropriate behaviour yourself, your first action should be to observe carefully the dynamics of the team and the behaviour of the dominant person. You have to be completely confident that this is a real issue.

### Dominant behaviour adversely affects teams

Once it is established that there is a real issue, you must address it, because the contribution to the team of the individual being dominated is bound to be affected. If the individual brings a particular skill or expertise to the team which you cannot afford to lose, it becomes even more imperative that you handle it straight away.

### Know what is and isn't acceptable

Everybody needs to know and agree what is acceptable and not acceptable. Every team will, to some extent, self-regulate: the irrepressible extrovert will generally be told by team members (through verbal feedback or non-verbal signals) when he or she is taking too much air time. However, agreeing a charter with the team will help everyone to contribute to defining what they find an acceptable working environment. Be sure that everyone has had an opportunity to contribute their views to developing this team charter. Agreeing a team charter with everyone's input doesn't necessarily mean that each individual has their views accepted by the team.

### Help people understand what you expect of them

Sometimes individuals will need to put aside their preferences to reflect the requirements of the culture agreed by the majority. Part of your responsibility is to translate the culture into commonly understood and accepted rules of behaviour. You also need to know who in the team will find these cultural rules difficult to observe.

### Individuals who dominate

One of the common behaviours that you might encounter which is not acceptable is that of the dominant individual. Dominant individuals tend to do more telling than asking and will often interrupt or override others in the group. It is sometimes the case that a team may have two or more dominant individuals who then become highly competitive. One of the first things you must decide is whether this inappropriate behaviour is conscious or unconscious. This decision will help you determine how to deal with it.

### Unconscious dominants

People who are unconsciously dominant may well respond to coaching. You may first wish to try unstructured coaching, through a light touch and informal conversation. If this doesn't get the response you need, you may need to suggest more formal coaching, either with you or with somebody else. The important thing is to agree with the individual what constitutes appropriate behaviour. Sometimes long-established habits that are unconscious are difficult to break and people need time and support to bring about behavioural change. A suggestion is to agree a covert signal between the pair of you so that you can make the individual aware of their behaviour as it's happening without anyone else knowing.

## Conscious dominants

Consciously dominant people tend to be overtly (even aggressively) competitive. They will be inclined to take on anyone who disagrees with them, making each conflict into a game of win or lose and not stopping until they have won. Because the behaviour of this type of individual is the result of a conscious choice, it is harder to get them to address it. It may not even be possible to do so and such people can be highly disruptive to team harmony and team performance.

One of the necessary decisions is whether such an individual can continue to have a place in the team. Sometimes this type of person will respond to a conversation about team and organisational goals, emphasising the need for sharing diverse perspectives in order to maximise team performance. Once you understand their personal ambitions you may also discuss with them the benefits of leading from the back (hearing everyone's views and having the patience and confidence to allow the team to reach a goal) versus leading from the front (being more concerned about your own views being heard or your own goals being met).

# Passionate or stubborn people

*Passion and stubbornness are emotional responses to a circum-stance. Resistance can often simply increase the same response. Until the circumstance is resolved there will be an impact on the performance and delivery of everyone involved. The management challenge is to facilitate the resolution.*

## First, think:

- What is your personal history with this individual? Do you *really* understand what they are stubborn or passionate about? Do you understand why they hold such views?

- Do you spend enough time with the people in your team or group to know why someone might feel especially stubborn about an issue? Is it possible to address any of this person's concerns?

- What effect is the behaviour of stubborn or passionate individuals having on the way the team or extended group works? Is the behaviour undermining any aspect of the team's culture and/or inhibiting the team's ability to meet objectives?

- When you are ready to address this problem, what is the best way to do so? How will you ask the individual to prepare for the meeting? How can you best prepare for such a meeting? What reactions might you expect to encounter?

- Would someone else have more chance of addressing and amending the behaviour than you would?

- Do you have access to dispassionate advice? Has anyone else found a way around this person's strong emotion?

# Ideas for action

## Know the people in your team as individuals

A critical skill for you as a manager is to know the people within your team so that the things about which they are passionate or stubborn are known to you long before they represent a barrier to progress. It is important that you understand and acknowledge your personal history with the individual concerned. Especially if you have a contentious past with them, you may find they put more barriers to progress than do team members with whom you have a harmonious history.

## Not all relationships can be perfect

If you've had a difficult relationship with a key team member or stakeholder, you can either address and attempt to resolve the issue or accept the consequences of a less than perfect relationship. If you've had a challenging past with the individual and want to improve the relationship, the best option is to do so through a private conversation in which both of you have the opportunity to speak openly about your past relationship and your hopes for your future relationship. If the relationship continues to be challenging and the team member consistently becomes passionate or stubborn about you, then you may need to ask others to influence the individual in an attempt to make progress.

Stubbornness is different from passion and is often the result of a person feeling undervalued or unheard. If it is possible that the individual legitimately feels this way, you have to work to change their perception. Passion, on the other hand, is often related to deeply held conviction. Persuading someone to change or modify a deep-seated conviction will take time. So, you need to be clear whether you have to change the conviction or merely acknowledge it.

## Understand that passion and stubbornness both impact on teams

One of your roles as manager is to notice the impact that extremes of behaviour have on the team as a whole. Often the people who have passionate or stubborn approaches do not realise the extent to which they are undermining team harmony, team cohesion and ultimately team effectiveness. Reminding the group of its pre-agreed team charter or having an off-line conversation with the stubborn or dominant individual are both potential ways to address this challenging issue. It's worth bearing in mind that behaviours that irritate you are almost certainly irritating others in the team as well. They may help you when you try to address the behaviours.

## Get good advice

Something else you might consider is to seek dispassionate advice from someone you respect who is well acquainted with you and with the individual whose behaviours you are finding challenging. You can explore how other people get on with this person. They may have ideas you have not yet thought of. Indeed, someone else may have found a way around this person's style which is currently foxing you. Don't be surprised if some of the advice you get relates to your own behaviour and how it affects the other person; indeed, you may find that it's you who are as passionate or stubborn as the individual who is proving to be so challenging – you might be as much a part of the problem as you are a seeker of the solution. Remember that your management challenge is to facilitate a positive resolution.

# 2

# Challenges with teams

This section and the chapters within it are full of solid advice on how to get the best out of teams, helping you to get under the skin of team dilemmas to make sure you are dealing with the right issue and dealing with it well. Managers who run teams will find the advice invaluable because it focuses on practical and pragmatic ways to deal with team-based dilemmas. Readers who are team members will be able to see some of the things that go wrong within their own team and ways to approach the causes of the problems.

Managing a team effectively and getting the best out of it is one of the biggest and most public challenges a manager can take on. There are so many ways in which team performance can be damaged or reduced, and you must be able to see each of them and deal with them before they get to the point where team performance is affected. Equally, by dealing with team issues swiftly and with a sure touch, good managers can give confidence to the team. This in turn will help the team to maximise performance.

This section will help you to spot some of the causes of a decline in team performance, such as issues of trust or the avoidance of conflict or accountability.

In teams where trust is reduced or has disappeared altogether, performance is highly likely to be compromised. But what is at the root of the trust issue? Is it something that has happened? Something that team members fear will happen? Is the lack of trust directed inwardly at team colleagues, outwardly at stakeholders, or even perhaps at the team's manager or leader? Is that you? Whatever the cause of the erosion of trust, your position means that you have to identify it and deal with it – and here's how.

Conflict, or the lack of it, within teams is another tricky area. Some conflict is bad, some is good. Sometimes conflict avoidance is the right strategy. But if the team is always unwilling to engage with conflict, then again team performance will be affected. What are the signs of conflict avoidance? How can you successfully address the issue? The answers are here.

# An under-performing team

*You lead a team which is under-performing. The team is measured by a number of metrics and is falling short on several of them. This reflects badly on you and you are experiencing pressure from above to act swiftly.*

## First, think:

- How long has this been going on? Is the decline accelerating, slowing or being reversed?
- How long have you been with the company? How well do you understand the way it works? Do you understand 'the way things are done around here'? How long have you been leading the team? What is your management style? How experienced and confident are you at management and leadership? Is this your first failing team?
- Are the metrics fair and appropriate? Does the team understand why and how they are measured?
- Is the team's performance dependent on the performance of other team(s) within or outside the organisation?
- Has the team undergone any major changes such as growth, contraction, or replacement of team members?
- What are the team dynamics? Do they get along with each other? Do they support and help each other? How do you deal with conflict?

# Ideas for action

## Under-performance is right at the root of management responsibility

Whatever you choose to do must address and turn around this under-performance. This is the time to be decisive and committed. All of this is more difficult if you have presided over the team while it has gone into decline. The longer the decline has gone on, the harder it is for all involved to turn it around and the worse it looks for everyone concerned.

## Establish facts, but act swiftly

Because this is so important, you want to establish as many facts and hear as many views as you can before you act. At the same time you must act swiftly. This issue should dominate your working days.

Decide what facts you need to establish and whose views you need to hear. First establish whether the metrics against which the team is being judged are fair and appropriate. If they are not, your first task is to establish and get approved a better set of metrics.

It may feel wrong to senior management to change agreed and established performance targets for a team, especially if that team is under-performing. So, if you genuinely feel that the metrics are wrong, you will need strong data-based arguments to support your position. What makes the metrics you want better than the metrics you have been given? Check your assumptions with a well-positioned mentor and be prepared for a challenging meeting with management where you must expect them to push back against your suggestions.

## Relationships can hinder performance

At the same time as examining metrics, you have to understand the relationships within the team. Are difficult relationships at the heart of the team's decline? High-performing teams are not only interdependent but also have high levels of mutual respect and a high desire to care for one another. If this is missing or in decline within the team then performance will suffer.

If you don't know enough about the relationships within the team, you must make it a priority to do so. Have you had the right balance between being task orientated and relationship orientated? A team in decline is a team in crisis. The style of management you choose is a vital element of the likely success or failure of your intervention.

The relationship you have had with your team thus far will influence the way you choose to try to lead the team out of this decline. If you haven't been a relationship-based leader, you can't become one overnight. But you must begin by taking a step or two in that direction so that you can start to build relationships for the long term. However, this won't be enough on its own and it won't have the immediate impact you need.

What about simple job competence? Is everyone able to do what they are supposed to do to the appropriate level? If you find there is a skills shortfall, you have to address it urgently.

## Nothing changes until you act

The turnaround you are looking for in team performance is unlikely to be achieved by your suddenly becoming much more hands-on and task orientated. It is much better if you also identify what is wrong with the team dynamics and deal with that.

# Lack of trust

*Trust is crucial for team development and team performance. Lack of trust can be seen in a variety of ways; often there is no outward conflict, yet team members behave formally and interact superficially with one another. A lack of trust will hold a team back from being the high-performing team it could be.*

## First, think:

- How does this team compare with the general standard within the organisation? Are they at, above or below the norm?
- Are there new team members or are they a long-established group? Have they ever performed better than they are performing now? If they have, what changed? Do you have any first thoughts about why there isn't more trust in the team? Do you suspect there may be conflict below the surface of the team?
- Who have you replaced and what style of team leadership did your predecessor use? What is your vision for this team?
- Do these people need to act interdependently or does each member have a specific, independent role?
- What is the team's working environment? Do they share an office space? Is it an open-plan office or do individuals have private work spaces? Or is it a virtual team?
- How much downtime does the team share? How often do they meet and for what purpose? Have they had any team development opportunities in the recent past?

# Ideas for action

## Groups versus teams: know the difference

The first thing to establish for yourself is whether you are leading a group or a team. A group is a collection of individuals who are aware of each other, who interact with each other and whose behaviour is influenced by shared interests or aspirations. A team goes beyond this: it is a number of people who share common objectives and need to work together to achieve those objectives.

A group will work side by side to achieve a task-based objective, whereas a team works interdependently and shares a common culture in order to address complex challenges. A high-performing team goes beyond this: they enjoy mutual trust and respect, many even say affection for one another.

## Helping groups to trust

If you are leading a group, focus on making sure each individual understands what they are to do and has the skills to do it to a high standard. Be sure that the individuals within the group communicates with one another more efficiently. In our experience almost all issues that arise in working groups are due to a lack of understanding of what the other people in the group do. Too often people fill gaps of understanding with assumptions.

## Helping teams to trust

The nature of businesses nowadays means that in the vast number of cases leaders will be leading teams, not groups. This is because the complex nature of organisational goals and structures means that for anything to be achieved, interdependent action will be needed.

Once you decide that you actually are leading a team then you need to focus on establishing trust and respect between and among team members. The degree to which you succeed will determine whether you lead an achieving team or a high-performing team.

## The prevailing culture affects trust and team performance

Teams rarely exist within a vacuum; they exist within organisational cultures. So, think about your organisation's attitudes to teams: are they valued and cherished? Does the organisation go out of its way to create and nurture high-performing teams or is a competent team good enough?

Even if the benchmark in your organisation is competence rather than high performance, don't let anything stand in the way of your creating your high-performance team. The first thing you'll need to do is convince your team that this is worth the effort. Create a vision, paint a story and appeal to their hopes and aspirations. Often individuals are attracted by emotions as much as by logic.

## Understanding the past will help you to manage the present

Before you try to make any changes you need to understand the team's history very clearly. It may be that in the past they have performed better than they are performing now. Or it may be that a previous leader has created a culture that created a barrier to high performance. Is it possible that internal conflict, changes in personnel and/or frustrated ambition (did someone apply for the job you have?) have contributed to the current culture? The best way to get under the skin of your team and answer these questions is to spend time with the individuals in the team and with the team itself.

## Have a clear vision about where you want to take the team

This will certainly involve ensuring high levels of trust and respect within the team. We trust people when we find them to be credible and reliable. Equally important but often forgotten is the need for openness: the team leader and the members of the team have to be brave enough to make themselves vulnerable to one another by sharing values and being honest about their own strengths, weaknesses and preferred ways of working. As leader, what you ideally want to get to is a team whose members care for one another.

## Self-orientation undermines trust

Something which significantly undermines trust is the sense that the other person is self-orientated in their decisions and actions. There are lots of ways in which individuals can be self-orientated: making decisions based on self-interest rather than team-interest; distributing workloads unfairly; claiming credit for others' work; avoiding difficult conversations or decisions because they find them challenging. One of your roles as leader is to identify and address the self-orientated actions of individuals. Trust builds slowly but can be destroyed quickly. However, trust lost can be regained, though this will take even more time. If you as leader model appropriately generous and forgiving behaviour, you give permission for others in the team to act in the same way.

We tend not to trust people we don't know well. At the root of much conflict is a lack of understanding of others at an individual level. So, the more time team members can spend working and getting to know one another, the more chance there is that trust will be created and mutual understanding developed.

## Trust can flourish when team members spend time together

Team-building days are an obvious option, but much can also be achieved simply by encouraging team members to spend time together brainstorming, reviewing, analysing and in other ways examining the business. Around this you can also build social opportunities, even if they are as straightforward as a sandwich lunch together.

Structured explorations of team profiles through the use of psychometric tools offer an excellent way to start conversations around how the team operates. The more diverse the group, the more value is to be had from this approach: it's often the very best way to understand the different skills and strengths that individual team members bring to the whole.

It is easy to underestimate the impact that office space can make on a team's culture. You may see a simple way to restructure or reorganise the space within the team's working environment to help foster a culture of collaboration and the exchange of ideas, information and opinions.

Trust is the issue of the decade. Life is complex, fast-paced and demanding; technology has facilitated a reduction in the amount of face-to-face time we spend with one another. A vital role for the leader is to create the time to spend together so that the trust we need can be built.

# Fear of allowing conflict in a team

*It can come as a surprise when a previously high-performing team starts to decline. In some teams this can happen because of conflict (which may or may not be openly discussed). However, if as an individual you value harmony and avoid conflict, it may be even more difficult for you to help the team address any underlying issues.*

## First, think:

- What is your definition of conflict? Does the team understand and share your definition?
- Do you value harmony over debate? Would your team enjoy a more robust and open culture?
- Have you had poor experiences in the past with conflict within teams? Is your approach to conflict similar in a professional and personal context?
- Are you seen to be (and do you think you are) assertive?
- How long has the team been together? How long have you been their manager? What is your relationship with the team?
- What about individuals in the team? What are their behavioural characteristics? Have you done any team profiling? Is everyone aware of what they bring (or can bring) to the team?

## Ideas for action

### Understand what you mean by conflict

Experts debate the definition of conflict, so it is important that you have a working definition. One approach is to say that conflict exists whenever opinions differ. With this approach, conflict is an everyday occurrence which should be embraced and used constructively. Another school of thought says that there is a difference between simple disagreements and real conflict which centres around value-based differences.

Within the first definition, discontent can be constructive and energising; it can be a catalyst for creative collaboration and for generating better solutions. The sort of conflict described in the second definition is unconstructive and potentially damaging to the relationships of the people involved. With this type of conflict nothing can progress until the conflict is resolved, and while the conflict exists a lot of the team's energy and momentum is dissipated.

Constructive discontent will not undermine harmony and should be allowed to flourish, because a team's most creative solutions will often flow from the energy of debate. Conflict where people feel their sense of self-worth is threatened or their principles are challenged is potentially harmful and must be managed carefully.

## Help others understand their own attitudes to conflict

It is quite common for people not to have a clear sense of their own attitude to conflict. A 360-degree assessment will tell you how others see your approach to conflict while your mentor or a trusted colleague can offer an individual, informed opinion. Sometimes people who value harmony too much do so because they feel they lack the ability to be assertive or they lack the ability to influence or guide a team. There are lots of ways to build these skills, with examples including struc-tured development courses, coaching, mentoring, reading management skills books. Often the difficulty is identifying the problem more than sourcing the solution.

If, on reflection, you realise that you deal with conflict very differently professionally than you do privately, think what you can learn from your approach to conflict away from work and how you might bring that learning to your professional environment. Once you are clear in your own mind, commit to accepting and generating what you now understand to be positive conflict.

## The past always informs the present

Make sure you have a very clear understanding of the team's history and how it has had an impact on the team's culture and achievements so far. Actively create opportunities to encourage discussion and debate within your team. Once you experience the benefits of encouraging constructive discontent you will want to make it a significant part of your management approach. Make sure your team understands the difference between positive exchanges of views and unconstructive, potentially harmful conflict. If you do have team members who are drawn towards unconstructive conflict – for example, someone who is aggressive, stubborn or highly opinionated – you must help them to understand that this type of behaviour is not constructive conflict and will not be supported.

## Encourage acceptable and constructive conflict

You may find you will need more team meetings and, within the meetings, more open-ended debates in which different views are encouraged. It might be an idea to rotate the facilitation of team meetings so that different leadership styles are experienced by team members. In addition, it's often helpful to have a clear idea of the strengths and preferences of your different team members. Profiling instruments help you to do this and some will also help you to explore specifically approaches to conflict.

You will also want to have more one-to-one (or one-to-few) meetings where you will encourage constructive exchanges. Open questions are a great way to generate a number of opinions which can then be discussed and debated in confidence, as team members know that any debate that takes place will be seen as positive and not as a sign of conflict.

## Conflict cannot be allowed to affect performance negatively

It is obviously vital to address any performance shortfall. If your new attitude to conflict seems to be working but performance is not improving, you need to re-examine your theory that your approach to conflict is at the root of the team's decline.

Above all, don't put your head in the sand: if your approach to conflict is holding back your team it will also be holding back your career. Take some positive steps to address the issue.

# A team that avoids accountability

*An important aspect of creating a high-performance team is ensuring that team members take accountability for their actions and performance. When a team is fragmented or relationships become brittle and, most importantly, when the service provided by the team is below the required standard, you must take action.*

## First, think:

- How does their avoidance of accountability manifest itself? When did the performance decline start? Was there a specific catalyst?
- What feedback have you had from the team? From the wider organisation?
- What have you already communicated to them with regard to service-level standards? Are individuals within the team clear about their role and contribution and where they should be accountable for delivery of results?
- How much team development has taken place so far? How have any outcomes been incorporated into how you work together?
- How aware are you of the detail of their daily tasks and responsibilities?
- Are there one or two individuals who generate animosity and tension in the team? Are there egos involved? Is there anyone for whom personal gain is more important than team gain? Who suffers most from the animosity?
- Who are the people in the team who are behaving and performing well?

# Ideas for action

## A low-performing team is clearly a problem team

We recognise that a problem exists when we experience the effects it creates; but to solve the problem we have to identify the cause. So here, the manager has to understand why the deviation from acceptable standards is happening. The error many managers make is to deal with the effects without attempting to identify and address the cause. This leads to an endless loop of solving the wrong part of the problem. Be strong. Managing a dysfunctional team out of their dysfunction (while still dealing with the team's operational responsibility from day to day) is difficult and exhausting. Bringing this team to a better place will require a judicious mix of authority and compassion.

## Dig deep

Take a close-up and critical look at how the team actually operates on a day-to-day basis. Who dominates? Who is work-shy? Who is withdrawn? Who has the power?

Familiarise yourself, too, with the details of their operational workload: what is each person supposed to do each day? What are the gaps between this and what they actually do? When and why are mistakes made? Is the workload balanced and fair?

Make sure you know the history of the team. How long have individuals been in post? Do any of the team members have an organisational history, good or bad, which might be relevant? Ask colleagues and trusted advisors for an objective external view of the team and its performance.

## Understand the limits of your authority

What can you do and not do? For example, do you have the authority to dismiss or reassign people? Can you restructure the team? Do you need more authority before you act and can you get it? Make sure, too, you understand your own standing within the team. Are you respected? Liked? Trusted?

## Address the performance-related effects

The team needs to acknowledge the standards to which they must perform and agree to deliver those standards immediately.

You must get to the root of what is causing the dysfunction within the team. It is likely to be multi-dimensional: keep turning over stones until you are sure you have left none unturned. Stones you will need to turn include examining the level of competence of each team member, and having one-to-one conversations with each member of the team to understand their challenges, frustrations and constructive suggestions. Listen also for positive things they want to keep.

## Start from scratch

Reset the team. Revisit any psychometric or team profiling that has been done and instigate some more. Take time with the team to build on team strengths and create a culture which is sustainable and which will lead to high performance. Trust will need to be a major component, as will an understanding of what is wrong with the current team culture. It is possible that an external facilitator would be helpful in maximising this opportunity.

## Look at the broader picture

Have the demands on the team changed unreasonably? Is the team doing too much or being asked to take on responsibilities for which they are not trained? When you identify things that are contributing to the team's dysfunction, don't be afraid to call it. If there are egos at play, if individuals are acting in their own interest, if there is bullying or discrimination, then these behavioural dysfunctions must be named and dealt with. However difficult this is, a dysfunctional team's problems can only be identified and addressed if you as the manager act bravely and directly.

## Create and champion clarity

You must also be sure that each team member has complete clarity about their own role and about the objectives of the team. The expectations that others (both internally and externally) have of the team must be identified, evaluated and, if they are appropriated, accepted. Once clarity is achieved, the team must accept that you will hold them accountable for delivering against the service-level agreements. This is best done on a one-to-one basis and then with the team as a whole.

## Be structured and systematic

There is a clear process here: you must deal with the performance shortfall as an immediate priority. At the same time (and this will take longer) you must find out the underlying causes and deal with them. If you only do one of these things, whichever one you do, it won't be enough. You will find that you are having a number of difficult conversations, both with individuals and with groups – sometimes with the whole team. If you don't feel equipped to do this then, before taking this challenge on, you need to get the support you require to enable you to undertake this demanding aspect of your role.

# Preferential treatment

*Managing a group of people can sometimes feel like being a parent. There can be accusations of preferential treatment, especially if you have a closer personal or professional relationship with an individual within the team. However, when resentment rises in the wider team and you hear accusations of preferential treatment being made, you must examine the situation to decide whether you are behaving fairly.*

## First, think:

- How stable is the team? Do members regularly quit and new members join?

- Who is the 'named individual' in the preferential treatment accusation? Is it someone with whom you have a close personal relationship? How long-standing is this friendship? How important is it to you? How do others know that you are friends?

- Is this individual a 'second-in-command' with whom you have a close working relationship? Is your deputy significantly more competent than everybody else in the team? Are there benefits (such as more money, longer breaks, less rigorous quotas, more varied workload) to being your informal second-in-command?

- Do others miss out on development opportunities because you regularly delegate to just one individual? Are there other training opportunities available to the team?

- How is the team performing generally? Are the accusations of preferential treatment coming only from the team or have you heard colleagues or supervisors suggesting or hinting at the same thing?

# Ideas for action

## Value friendship properly

Friendships at work are both natural and healthy. We spend more time at work than we do at home, so to treat it as a friendless environment would be unnatural. Nevertheless, how others perceive your friendships at work is important, particularly if you are in a position of power or authority. Managers are very closely observed by the people they manage. If you are thought to be favouring one individual, it will naturally lead to resentment which in turn will have a negative impact on team performance.

Remember that someone else's perception of events is their reality and their truth. You have to accept and deal with this perception even if it seems unfair or inaccurate to you.

You need to step back and assess the quality of your friend's professional contribution. Is he or she significantly better than the other members of the team? If not, is there perhaps something in the resentment that others feel? Think too about how many people in the team appear to have strong feelings about this issue. Is it widespread or isolated to two or three individuals? Have people outside the team commented or even criticised the relationship with your friend and the informal role you have given him or her? A widespread concern suggests a genuine issue. Concern limited to a small number of individuals may suggest personal agendas.

When you are a manager, even if the answer is not what you want it to be, it is important that you address the real issue.

## Take a step back

With a mentor's help you can take a step back and objectively analyse the situation. Do you treat this individual preferentially? Are others aware of (and uncomfortable with) your close personal relationship? What is the nature of their discomfort? Is it the time you are spending with this individual (which takes time away from other team members)? Is it an uneven distribution of job responsibility?

Nobody likes to hear criticism of themselves or their friends. However, if your mentor does believe that some of the resentment is justified, you owe it to your team to consider carefully the informal structure you have created. Another way to approach this is to look at the team you are leading. Are they content or unhappy? Stimulated or bored? Busy or idle? If people are idle then gossiping and speculation may fill the idle time.

## Where is the source of the discontent?

You must identify and deal with the root cause of the discontent in your team. There are only two possibilities: with the team or with your relationship. If you feel the root cause lies with the team, then you need to work with the team to address what is fundamentally a cultural issue. If, however, the root cause lies with the relationship between you and your friend then you need to review and address the responsibility and authority you delegate to him or her.

## Perceptions of preferential treatment can lead to performance decline in teams

If team performance is in decline then this issue has taken a serious hold. Even if the team's performance is holding up, do remember that a shift in attitude (which you may not notice) will generally precede a shift in behaviour (which you will notice) as it leads to performance decline.

Relationships at work must be fundamentally professional. We all need and want friendships in the workplace. Indeed, many of us work better when our working environment includes people we count as friends. However, when your relationships become too exclusive (with private jokes or frequent downtime together) then everyone else in your team feels left out.

People in the team who might feel that your relationship with your friend is denying them the chance to progress or withholding developmental opportunities may well be justified in their resentment. You may feel you have been discreet in how you have managed your relationship. However, people in your team will be watching you very carefully and will be quick to spot examples of inequity, however much you disguise them.

## Observe and decide – objectively

The nature of a Number 2 role is that the person in that role generally undertakes the role in your absence. This means that your view of their ability may not align with the team's experience of their ability. It is important both to observe the Number 2 in action (more than once if possible) and to seek feedback from the team on his or her performance.

Keep in mind that there are two challenges here: one is that when you observe you change the dynamic and you cannot be sure that what you are observing is what would happen were you not there. The second challenge is that the relationship itself may be a barrier to your getting objective and honest feedback from the team.

Objectively, if your friend is not a good manager and is not the most suitable deputy manager then he or she should not be given the role or opportunity. If there is nobody who is more suited to the role then your friend should, at the very least, be given the training and development needed to take the role on properly.

Management can be lonely. It's often difficult for managers to have close friendships with members of their own team. By its nature the role of a manager is to stand apart and be objective; you can't lead the team and be a team member. If this issue boils down to a simple choice, will you risk the team to keep the friendship or risk the friendship to support the team? The answer to this question will tell you a lot about your approach to your career as a manager.

# Silo mentality

*Sometimes well-established teams can see themselves as separate and different from the rest of the organisation. Over time these teams can develop a mentality which is compartmentalised, either due to a competitive spirit or because they feel nobody understands them or what they do. This unhealthy behaviour can create tension within the organisation. Your role as their manager is to ensure they see the bigger picture and to help the team better integrate into the wider organisation.*

## First, think:

- Is it acceptable to have this kind of culture within the organisation? What has helped to create the culture of silo thinking? What makes you sure this is the wrong culture for this group?
- What are the benefits of better integration? Who within the team would resist it? Who would support the integration?
- What are the compensation structures within your organisation? Do they support silo thinking? How is the team judged? Who sets the performance standards?
- How are the team performing? Are delivery targets being met?
- Has something triggered your concerns about the team culture? What is your management style? How competitive are you?
- How often does the team need to interact with and partner with other departments? Who do they see as their client? What, if anything, are the team's stakeholders saying about the team?

- How interested and informed are the team about other departments or the organisation as a whole?
- Do the team members feel valued?

# Ideas for action

## Insularity hinders effectiveness

The challenge with silo mentalities is that they create insularity within an organisation. Organisations work best when inter-dependent action is easy to generate and maintain. Every organisation is complex; the larger the organisation the harder it is to step back and see how all the different aspects of the organisation work together. Even if your team appears to work efficiently, creating opportunities to interact with other elements of the organisation will help to generate a more integrated whole.

## Size matters

The larger the organisation the more important it is to pay attention to how teams are structured, how people are paid and even what is discussed during team meetings. Are teams structured vertically? Are teams paid solely for their own contribution or are they at least in part remunerated for their ability to engage with and interact with other parts of the organisation? Are team meetings only about team perfor-mance and team issues or do they also incorporate broader organisational goals? The more commonality there is across departments the more likely it is that important aspects of the big picture will be shared and understood.

For a team to be integrated within the wider organisation it must see its role within the larger picture and not in a vacuum. Managers of teams have a responsibility to represent the team within the organisation and to represent the organisation to the team. This means that it's the manager's job to make sure that the organisation understands and respects the contri-bution the team makes and to make sure the team understands the role it has in the wider operations of the organisation.

## Make your team feel valued by you and by others

As part of your reflection on why the team has a silo mentality you should think about whether they feel truly valued by you and the organisation. Teams that feel undervalued can sometimes appear arrogant because they are defensive about their contribution or status within the organisation. The more people (both within the team and within the wider organisation) are anxious about your team becoming isolated and insular, the better your chances of changing this attitude. If you are a lone voice and your concerns are not shared, you will find it significantly more difficult to challenge the team's attitude.

## Find and use others who share your views

An early action point is to identify people (within and outside your team) who share your view that your team is isolated and share your determination to end that isolation. Ideally these people will be stakeholders and in positions of authority and influence. You can take advice from these people and together form a plan to better integrate your team. If people don't share your view, reflect on whether your opinion is sound in the context of how your organisation operates. Sometimes it isn't enough to be right: you need other people to support your views. As a manager you will find there are always plenty of battles to fight; sometimes the trick is to know which battles to choose.

If your department is performing well, meeting targets and generally doing all that is asked of them, it will be more difficult to encourage people to address what can readily be dismissed as a non-problem. If the organisation or the team itself is content with performance levels, then nothing short of a sharp shock or a compelling new vision may be required to convince people that there is any need to assess current attitudes.

If, upon reflection, you decide you would like to fight this battle, you will need support. If you don't have enough people with influence who share your view, you will need to find ways to convince them that yours is an appropriate position to take. Without some support you will find your position untenable.

## Understand the attraction of the silo mentality

Can you isolate why your team feels more comfortable working in a silo? Was there a particular incident or individual who caused a shift in attitude? Has there been a long-term, gradual decline into isolation? The answers to these questions will give you clues to the exact cause of the problem and therefore potential actions. If you are well established as the team's manager, you will have contributed to the team's culture. If you are competitive, you may have encouraged your team to compete internally. Or perhaps you have been too critical about other teams within the organisation. In either case the end result might be that the team has mirrored your style.

The team's culture and attitude will depend largely on how they see themselves. For example, do they see themselves as serving the organisation or serving the organisation's customers? An integrated team will see their customer as being both the internal organisation and the external recipient. An isolated team will pay more attention to the external recipient than to the internal client.

A good yardstick is to consider team meetings. Do the team want to spend the time thinking and talking about their role within the organisation or are they more likely to focus on other external issues and demands and how these affect their ability to perform efficiently and effectively? An integrated team will want to consider both internal and external challenges and opportunities.

# Managing a virtual team

*Managing virtual teams is becoming increasingly commonplace, yet many managers have minimal experience and understanding of how to communicate, develop and lead virtually. The complexities of managing a virtual team can lead to a team that is fragmented and disengaged, which in turn is likely to have an impact on team performance.*

## First, think:

- How familiar are you with the demands of running a virtual team? How experienced in virtual team working are the people in the virtual team?
- How good is your technology? How good is the technology in each of the countries where you operate? Is everything compatible?
- Does your management style differ between the team you sit with and the virtual team?
- How often do you actually meet the individuals in the virtual team? Do they come to you or do you go to them? Do you choose to interact virtually rather than making the effort to travel to different locations? Do you resent or regret the time you are required to spend travelling or to spend in virtual meetings which take place outside normal working hours?
- How well do the team know each other? How often does the team communicate as an entire group? How often do they come together face to face?
- How well do you understand the culture, customs and practices of the different countries where you have team

members? How many are using a second or third language when communicating to the wider team?

# Ideas for action

## Virtual teams are different

Virtual team working is difficult, and the difficulties are not the same as those encountered in face-to-face team working. It is inevitable that more and more managers will have a virtual component to deal with as business becomes ever more global. However, virtual team working is challenging in many ways.

## Harness technology

One of the complications is the technology required to maximise team effectiveness. This technology is evolving and constantly changing. In addition, the stance of your company on investment in technology and spend on travel will significantly affect the quality of your virtual management.

When choosing and using technology remember that virtual meetings will always be improved if the participants can see each other. Make webcams central to your approach to technology. Most of us are not aware of just how much we use our senses when we interact with people face-to-face. Virtual interaction means that you cannot use all of these senses, so the two that you can use (sight and hearing) are even more important.

Of our five senses our eyesight dominates over all others. If we are on the telephone our eyes can distract us, drawing our attention to other things (such as a PC screen or even the view from the window). The same thing can happen in a meeting if we become bored or disinterested, so if you want the people you are interacting with to pay you high-quality attention it is really important to give them the ability to make eye contact with you. It's not just about their attention; the quality of the relationship will also be better if you can see each other.

An important dimension provided by being able to see each other is that people can see how others are reacting to what they are hearing and can get a better-nuanced understanding of how the message is landing. Whatever sort of team you are managing, paying attention to the people is as important as paying attention to the task. But with a virtual team, in our opinion, you need to focus on the relationship even more than on the task, particularly because there is a temptation to interact with virtual team members only when there is a specific, task-related reason to do so.

## Don't compromise

Even though it is more difficult with virtual teams, you must set yourself the same exacting standards around critical success factors such as motivating and inspiring the team. When that team is a blend of virtual and same-space, the management challenges can be even tougher.

## Relationships matter even more with virtual teams

Of primary importance is the need to form and maintain high-quality relationships with everyone in the team, whether they work virtually or in the office next door. Seize every opportunity to meet your team face-to-face. Make specific trips if you can, but certainly prioritise attendance at gatherings like sales conferences or regional meetings if they offer a chance to meet your virtual team face-to-face.

You have to be able to inspire, motivate and engage individuals and teams virtually just as you have to with face-to-face teams. Use stories, imagery, anecdotes, metaphors – anything which will stimulate your virtual team and encourage them to connect with you and the other team members. You will need to build bridges between the element of the team that works virtually and the element that shares your office space. It's important that they are seen as one team, not two. If you don't have a strategy around this, the risk is that the team will become 'we' and 'they' rather than 'us'. One simple thing you could do is create a networking platform where all the team members can interact synchronously and asynchronously.

## Virtual teams usually mean cultural diversity

You have a responsibility to understand the huge amount of cultural diversity that exists in most virtual teams: for example, an Asian sales director may be working for a European organisation and representing them in an African country. Your responsibility is to understand all of these cultural backgrounds. The need for you to show informed flexibility is even greater as a virtual manager.

## Understand the blended teams challenge

A challenge you have to accept is that many people find it easier to build and maintain face-to-face relationships. So, if one of your team has, for example, a dotted relationship in-country, that relationship may well be stronger and easier to maintain than the direct-line but virtual relationship with you. The ease of that relationship may be aided by factors such as cultural alignment, proximity and the ease of social interaction. One result may be an unintentional distortion of the reporting line.

There is a temptation for virtual teams to fragment into factions, perhaps based on cultural and geographical alignments, rather than on any business-based rationale. This can hinder the efficiency of the team and you will need to spend time interacting with team members individually in order to break down these invisible walls and maintain the integrity of the larger group.

## Different ways of working

It is important to establish respectful ways of working. Map out the time zones represented in your team and identify workable time windows when you can meet synchronously. Map out the working days (bearing in mind holidays and differences in weekends) to identify workable days for the entire team. Virtual team meetings need to be carefully planned and executed. Material that needs to be discussed must be circulated well in advance; extra time needs to be built into the meeting when some or all participants are talking and listening in a language other than their mother tongue. Make sure you establish strong feedback loops so that you can be sure that what works for you is also working for all your team members.

## The dynamics of virtual meetings

Virtual meetings differ significantly from face-to-face meetings. For example, you will need to be more comfortable with silence. Attendees need more time to understand, to reflect, to gather their thoughts and to contribute than is typically the case in face-to-face meetings. Be sure you really do have agreement before you move on. It is also significantly more difficult to make sure you are getting contributions from everybody involved in the meetings, because you can't make the same generalised eye-contact or review the mood of the room as readily when the room is a virtual room.

## Be clear about the nature of the team you are managing

Is it permanent or temporary? Is it a working group with a number of specific, independent tasks or is it a team with real, shared objectives? If you are managing a temporary project group then you may find more resistance to the time, energy and commitment required to work successfully virtually. In temporary project groups you often need to work harder to help team members discover what's in it for them, rather than simply to recognise what's in it for you.

Managing virtual teams can and should be as rewarding and exciting as managing real-time teams. It really is the case that the more effort you put in the more rewarding it becomes.

# Meetings that stagnate

*Meetings are vital in any organisation but nobody enjoys an inefficient meeting. People who are regularly late for meetings or quit meetings before the end often do so because they do not have respect for the way the meeting is being run or what the meeting is discussing. Even the best-run meetings can stagnate at some point. A key people skill is to notice the subtleties in meetings so you can re-engage, re-energise and regenerate momentum.*

## First, think:

- This challenge is as much about being able to react in the moment as it is about planning: how good are you at observing and assessing before acting swiftly? Are you good at interpreting body language? Do you know who among the participants is more extrovert and who will need to be coaxed into contributing? Do you have a sense of who might readily become bored or distracted?

- Are you an experienced meeting chair? If not, would you consider either encouraging someone better equipped to chair this meeting or perhaps rotating the chair role in order to create and maintain momentum?

- What distractions are there likely to be in the meeting? Will attendees have tablets, phones, laptops or other electronic gear turned on?

- How well have you planned the meeting? Have you sent out material in advance? Have you allowed enough time for each agenda item or to meet the objectives of the meeting?

- If there are set presentations on the meeting agenda, what can you do to ensure the speakers are well prepared with an engaging presentation?
- Is the meeting predominantly about assessing and understanding data, or more about discussing complex issues where different opinions are bound to exist? Is it a meeting to ratify the decisions of others? Can you build reasonable breaks into a longer meeting?

# Ideas for action

## Get skilled in meeting management

Generally, the first things people want to consider are their meeting chairing and facilitation skills and you will no doubt want to be confident in these skills. Many organisations are very meeting orientated and it has become increasingly vital to develop constantly your chairing and facilitation skills. Beyond these skills, you also need to hone the more subtle skills such as your ability to observe the people in the room: who is bored, who is disengaged, who has lost focus. It's these people who cause meetings to stagnate. Don't be afraid to ask others who will be in the meeting to help you observe. You will want to ask people you can trust. This is easier when you know well the people attending the meetings; it's more difficult when you are in meetings with unfamiliar people.

Different organisations have different customs around electronic equipment. Electronic devices can be incredibly disruptive during a meeting: when they are turned on, whatever benefits they bring, they also present a risk because people find them very distracting. However, in many organisations it is now accepted that these devices can and will be constantly used in meetings. If this is the case in your organisation, your responsibility is to manage their use discreetly so that the meeting gets the benefits but not the disadvantages.

## Make sure a meeting is the best mechanism

A necessary challenge that you should set yourself is to ask whether this meeting is really necessary or whether a meeting is the best way to get to the outcome you require. The culture in some organisations is biased towards meetings, but even here the question should be asked. Once you've determined that your meeting is necessary, you need to ensure you have prepared fully. Poorly prepared meetings or meetings without clear agendas are likely to stagnate. Be sure that you have done your homework in advance of each meeting so that you and the attendees are clear about the objectives. Send out lists of pre-reading and actions required by individuals in advance wherever possible. Keep the meeting as short as possible while maintaining an atmosphere where everyone's viewpoint is heard. You will lose people's attention if you go down rabbit holes or allow an individual or a single issue to dominate the meeting.

Meetings can also stagnate when some of the people in the meeting feel that they could be making a better contribution by doing something else somewhere else. Perhaps they have an urgent deadline or a big project reaching fruition which is diverting their attention. It's always difficult to keep people's attention when something they believe is important is going on elsewhere.

## Make meetings rewarding experiences

A way to pre-empt meeting stagnation is to pursue a policy of continuous refreshment. Encouraging constant feedback, new ideas for how the meeting should be run, and having a team charter for behaviours in the meeting can help to avoid stagnation. Attendees are more likely to feel committed to positive outcomes if they have had input to how the meetings are run. Also, meeting outcomes are more likely to be positive if people's expectations of meeting content and meeting behaviours are established in advance of the meetings themselves.

If you are running a meeting in which people are making formal presentations, you will want to reassure yourself that these are well prepared and will be well delivered. Presentations which are not can quickly cause a meeting to stagnate. If time allows, try to make yourself available to help more junior attendees to refine their presentation or delivery. This will have two benefits for you: it will ensure your meeting runs with more energy and it will add to your credibility as a leader within your organisation.

## Poor meeting management can lead to stagnation

People need regular breaks and need to know when to expect them. Particularly if your meeting content is detailed or complex, having regular breaks and, if appropriate, refreshments to hand, can help maintain energy levels.

Too many meetings become stagnant because of a lack of preparation or forethought on the part of the meeting owner. If you make it your personal responsibility to ensure that your meetings do not stagnate, there is a lot you can do both before and during the meeting to make sure that energy levels are established and maintained throughout.

# Meetings that derail

*A meeting that derails is a meeting whose objective is missed or set aside because of something that happens within the meeting. Derailment could be caused by interpersonal friction or by the meeting unearthing an issue which is both unexpected and urgent. Good planning, preparation and meeting management can minimise the risk of derailment, but equally important is to know how to deal with it when you can't prevent it.*

## First, think:

- How prepared are you for derailment? Do you understand as well as you can what the attendees' views and feelings are about the agenda contents or the meeting's stated objectives? Are there points in the meeting where these are likely to differ significantly from your own?

- What could you do before the meeting to address this risk with the individual or group who you fear may derail the meeting?

- Can or should you override the derailment attempt? If not, what effect will it have on the rest of the agenda and on other attendees?

- Is there a hidden agenda that is emerging? If so, is it a personal agenda or one to do with the individual's organisational role or position? Does interpersonal friction play a part – is this derailment attempt part of a different battle?

- If you do not oppose the derailment, what will you say to the meeting to make sure that everyone else is prepared to allow this shift in direction?

# Ideas for action

## No excuses: plan and prepare

Some people simply find planning and preparation tedious. When you add in the pressure of work that many people experience and the increasingly frenetic schedule people have, the end result is that it is much too easy to avoid planning and preparation. Unfortunately it is difficult and dangerous to approach meetings spontaneously and expect to get the outcome that you want.

Experience will tell you that time spent in preparation is never time wasted, or, as has often been said, 'failing to prepare is preparing to fail'. Make sure, for example, that you have thought about things like the type of meeting that you are having and the people who are attending: do you know what you want from the meeting and do you know what they might think about this outcome? Do you have an agenda planned and circulated? Do you know what the contentious areas of the meeting might be? Do you know the individual personalities and the group dynamics that will be in the room? When you think about it in this way, you will swiftly see that there is a great deal of preparation that needs to be done.

## Identify and address issues pre-meeting

Having thought things through, you may well find there is a need before the meeting to address something which otherwise may be an issue within the meeting. This might mean having an offline discussion with one of the attendees to smooth the way. Even if this offline discussion doesn't resolve the issue, it does at least help you to prepare for the objections you are likely to hear in the meeting.

## Assess the benefits of derailment

Within the meeting itself, if you do encounter an attempt to derail the meeting, you need swiftly to consider whether the unexpected issue or insight or opposition is indeed urgent enough to allow the derailment. If at the heart of the derailment is a significant business issue which is both urgent and important, think about the team's and/or the organisation's goals and objectives: are these better met by allowing the derailment and pursuing the issue or by resisting it and keeping to the meeting's stated purpose and agenda? You must also quickly decide what is behind the derailment attempt so that your response is appropriate.

## Meetings don't happen in a vacuum

Generally, all of the attendees have a history with one another. Into the meeting comes the friction of past encounters and the emotional baggage of interpersonal relationships. Often there are undercurrents, particularly in teams where individuals are vying for position and influence. A frequent issue is the lack of respect that some team members may have for others, based on past experiences and past impressions. These undercurrents will always affect the way people respond to the views, opinions, suggestions and recommendations of others.

Your responsibility in running the meeting is to make sure that none of these pre-existing tensions are allowed to derail the meeting or to affect it to the point where decisions are compromised. Being prepared is important, but in the meeting itself, the skill of facilitation is just as valuable. Every voice must be heard but none should dominate; the agenda should be followed and timekeeping must be judicious. Part of your role is to give credit for positive contributions while knowing when to exert control over somebody whose contributions are less helpful.

## Anticipate self-interest and hidden agendas

Sometimes meetings derail because individuals are drawn towards their own area of personal interest at the expense of addressing the actual issue under discussion. This is about people being happiest in their comfort zones and your role is to make sure there is a tight focus on the subjects you really need to explore. This is where a clear agenda is useful.

Hidden agendas can be personal or professional and by their very nature are hard for you to spot. For example, someone might attempt to avoid being given extra work by suggesting that another attendee is well suited to the responsibility. If you do think someone is pursuing their own agenda, you can either call them on it or, by constantly reminding the attendees of the published agenda, let the individual know that their hidden agenda will not be permitted.

If you have explored all of these avenues and still feel concerned that your meetings are not successful, you may want to reflect on this: some organisations have a meetings-based culture. Too many meetings are called when better solutions exist. Meetings that lack focus or purpose swiftly lead to participants becoming bored. Attention levels will drop while levels of dissatisfaction will rise. So before you call your meeting, ask yourself this simple question: is a meeting with these people the very best way to address and resolve this agenda?

# 3

Challenges with externals

Clients, suppliers and partners have some right to
shift the goalposts – after all, their world can be
volatile and challenging as well. However, if this is
taken to extremes, then your ability to manage your
team and to deliver against expectations can be
seriously undermined. You'll have to deal with this
inappropriate treatment, and it is a sensitive area
where you'll need to tread carefully. Do it right, and
both your team and your stakeholder will respect
you and your management skills – here's the advice
that will help you consider the right things and then
act in the best way.

Today's managers often have to deal with complex
stakeholder dynamics, and often some of the most
significant players are clients, suppliers and partners.
Managers, especially those in service industries,
may regularly have to deal with sensitive dilemmas
around unrealistic behaviour, unresponsive behaviour,
arrogance or constantly changing goalposts.

This is difficult territory for managers, as you are in
your forward-facing role where often you can be seen
as representing the entire company. At times you can
hold a vital relationship in the palm of your hand, so
any wrong move can be costly for your organisation
and damaging for your own credibility and career
prospects.

When the stakes are that high, you will feel better and more confident for having good advice behind you. This section looks at the sort of unrealistic expectations that clients or customers can have, how to address them and how to make sure that unfair or inappropriate demands are not being made on your team. We also look at clients who are difficult to pin down, or reluctant to respond to you or give you the decisions or permissions you need.

Many managers have to deal with external stakeholders who can be patronising or arrogant. It's important that you can do this without generating tension or aggression – but deal with it you must, or you will help to create a client who has little respect for you and by extension for your team and your organisation.

# Their unrealistic expectations

*You have a business relationship with an organisation which regularly sets very demanding deadlines for you to respond to complex requests. However, they themselves take a lot of time to respond to your questions or requests, regularly missing deadlines you try to impose. Your contact describes your working relationship as a partnership; to you it feels like a master/servant relationship.*

## First, think:

- What is the nature of this relationship? Are you a service provider? A supplier? A customer? A stakeholder? Is an equal partnership a credible option?
- What is your relationship like with your contact? What do you think he or she thinks of the relationship?
- How does this relationship compare with the way you do business with other similar organisations?
- What impact does the client behaviour have on your team and on your wider organisation?
- What do other stakeholders in your organisation think about the way this client behaves? Do other people also find their expectations to be unrealistic?
- How much do you know about their organisational culture and their way of working? Has something changed to exert particular pressure on the individual or on the organisation?

# Ideas for action

### Reasonable behaviour is a minimum standard

It is important within any business relationship that you have reasonable expectations of that relationship. Many successful business relationships are not based on the premise of both parties being equal; instead within what is a service mentality, there exists mutual respect. In this type of relationship, you may find that a more attainable aim is one of mutual respect.

### Mutual respect helps to sustain relationships

A business relationship where mutual respect is important but does not exist is probably not sustainable in the long term. Relationships where this respect is important but lacking will always be vulnerable to competitors who can build a mutually respectful relationship. For example, a paint manufacturer who is the sole supplier of a unique metallic paint to a car manufacturer but who does not have a good-quality relationship with their client is only secure until another provider can offer a similar product.

Purely transactional relationships won't require this respect: for example, a pharmaceutical company may have a purely transactional relationship with their stationery supplier but may want a mutually respectful relationship with their supplier of raw materials. So it is vital that you are honest with yourself about the quality and nature of your relationship.

### Don't expect perfection

The first thing to decide is whether you're going to take any action, and if so, what that action will be. No relationship is perfect and, particularly if you are a service provider, there are some things you just have to accept.

The next thing to decide is whether your issue is with the individual involved or the organisation: does the behaviour you dislike represent the organisation's norm or is it something specific to the person with whom you have a relationship? There is more leeway with an individual than with an organisation.

## Be realistic and objective about what the relationship will bear

It is easier to be open with people whom we have known for a while. So, challenging practices which we don't like with someone we know well is easier than doing this with someone new. Bear in mind too that relationships take time to form and mature. This situation may just be the result of teething problems. Similarly, new appointees often want to impress their own colleagues and managers; the individual may feel the best way to do this is to take a hard line with you.

It is possible that it is the person who has rubbed you up the wrong way rather than the situation. We don't get along with everyone in equal measure and a sign of a good manager is to be able to build good working relationships even with people we don't particularly like.

It is important to get some objectivity. Ask a trusted colleague for their views: do others see the behaviour in the same way you do? Think about other clients or customers: how do they behave and what demands do they make? Do you have experience from previous roles or jobs which help tell you whether these demands are inappropriate or out of sync? These are demanding times and in such times we must expect clients or customers to be demanding too.

## Don't be the fool who rushes in...

If you do decide to take action you might initially try some low-risk, subtle tactics. For example, you may wish to use email correspondence or an informal telephone call to draw attention gently to unnecessarily tight deadlines. Or if you suspect it is the individual who is making unreasonable demands you may try implicating the organisation rather than the individual. You might say to your client, 'Is there any leeway to this deadline your organisation has put forward?' or 'How do you find having to work with such tight deadlines?' This allows the individual to reconsider their demands without feeling they have been personally criticised and therefore defensive.

It is probably obvious that you wouldn't approach a client or partner with a list of complaints. At the same time you do want to address the issue and there are times when a more formal conversation is warranted. A good way to start is with open questions such as, 'How are you finding working together?', 'Are there any things about how we work together that you'd like to change or review?', 'This relationship is important. Should we incorporate feedback as part of how we regularly review the business?' This allows you to hear the client's point of view before expressing your own concerns. It also allows you to give some positive feedback of your own before offering some constructive critical comments.

Before you initiate this conversation you should be sure to have some positive suggestions of your own about how to improve the working relationship. The suggestions should be specific, realistic and constructive.

### ...but you have to be prepared to take risks

If you genuinely feel you have exhausted every avenue in seeking to improve the situation, a high-risk option may be to discuss what is happening with a stakeholder in your client organisation. You may discover that you are not alone in finding a relationship with this individual difficult. Equally, you may get feedback which helps you to see the situation in a different light. It's risky because you may be seen as a whistle-blower who is blowing the whistle on somebody in another organisation. But it may provide a good, useful alternative especially if your relationship with the stakeholder in that organisation is a strong one and if taking no action would jeopardise the business your organisation has with this client.

# Elusive or unresponsive behaviour

*It is difficult to maintain high levels of performance when your supplier or client does not respond as you would expect. If they are late answering your queries via email or voicemail messages, the knock-on effect to you can be big: decisions you need to make will be delayed because the information you require is not forthcoming.*

## First, think:

- What is the nature of this relationship? Are you a key account for your supplier? Does your supplier provide an important or unique service or product?
- Is this unusual behaviour or is it the norm? If it is unusual, can you identify what might have changed? Do you know of reasons why your supplier might be distracted?
- Are you confident that you have communicated with clarity the decisions and timescales required by your organisation? Are you asking too much of your supplier? Could you do more to help them provide their service or information to you?
- What is your individual relationship like with your key point of contact? Are either of you aloof, self-contained or formal in the relationship?
- Is it possible that this is an unprofitable or low-margin account for your supplier? Have the terms and conditions of your contract with them changed recently? Do you have a sense of where you lie on their priority list?

- Are there any other relationships between your company and this supplier? If so, how are those relationships faring? Is this supplier well regarded across your organisation?

# Ideas for action

## Take a step back

If this unresponsiveness is unusual or out of character, the first thing you can do is increase your attempts to make personal contact with your supplier. If you can't make contact with your supplier, you could try to get a sense of what's going on through another contact at their organisation. You may find the supplier has valid personal reasons; equally, there might be business reasons why you aren't getting a reply. For example, an acquisition may be on the cards, a round of redundancies might be happening, or industrial action might be taking place.

Next, determine where the power lies in this relationship. You need to understand how important the relationship is for each party. For example, a big supplier with a unique product may unintentionally pay less attention to smaller clients than to their largest customers. Part of your responsibility is to understand the exact nature of the relationship between the two parties and manage your expectations accordingly. You may need to accept that you and your organisation need this supplier more than they need you.

If this elusiveness is the norm and you find it unacceptable behaviour in a supplier, you need to plan how you will raise this with the supplier organisation. If you do take this route, be clear on what you want and come prepared with specific suggestions on how things can improve. At the same time, you may wish to begin evaluating options such as alternative suppliers.

Finally, if this elusiveness is the norm but the client holds the power in the relationship, you could choose to do nothing. If the client holds all of the cards and the business is important to your organisation, you may decide it is too potentially risky to upset the client.

## You have to act reasonably and responsibly

Make sure the demands you are making are reasonable, clear and appropriate. For example, look for ways in which you can make your systems and processes supplier-friendly; make sure all your communications are unambiguous. Make sure you are allowing the supplier to make a reasonable margin which allows them to service your business properly.

## Don't be afraid to be assertive

If you believe the problem centres on the relationship and especially if you believe you hold the power in the relationship, then you should feel able to address this issue openly. Have a frank exchange of views and, if you see no improvement, bear in mind that you could ask for an alternative contact point from your supplier.

If you find that the relationship is failing but you want to keep the supplier, you may want to delegate the relationship to someone in your team who you think might be better suited to manage it. You shouldn't see this as a failure: interpersonal chemistry is always difficult to anticipate and manage.

## Learn from others

If your organisation holds multiple relationships with this supplier, seek out colleagues who interact with this organisation and exchange experiences. This will help you to decide whether this is an individual or a cultural issue. If you find that this unresponsiveness characterises this supplier's behaviour across your organisation, then it is a strategic issue which you and your colleagues together need to bring to the attention of senior management.

## Buyers have choices

If you really don't think you are an important enough account for this supplier, you should shop around for alternative suppliers. Sometimes smaller suppliers may be hungrier and more determined to service your business really well.

# Patronising or arrogant styles

*It is difficult to maintain a positive and professional working relationship with someone who treats you in a patronising way. Sometimes people with this type of personality become arrogant and even aggressive if you resist or offer an alternative point of view. If this is an important relationship, you need to find a solution in order to redress the balance.*

## First, think:

- When you are in disagreement with this person, how confident are you of your ground and of the views you are expressing? Does this person trust you and see you as competent?

- Is this person's behaviour any different when there are other people in the meetings? Does this individual behave with other people as they behave with you?

- What triggers the outbursts? Is it what you say or how you say it? When they are patronising or aggressive towards you, what has your reaction been?

- Are you more upset about how this person speaks to you or about the content of what is being said?

- What is the internal perception of this individual and of their behaviour? Does anyone else share the same difficulty with their style as you? Is the person under particular pressure to perform or to deliver?

- Is there anyone who can share the management of the relationship with you, or even take it over altogether?

# Ideas for action

## Every relationship is two-way

There is your relationship with the individual and that individual's relationship with you. Behaviour does not happen in a vacuum and is generally triggered by something. Even in situations where you don't agree with the response you have received or the way in which it has been given, you still need to take a critical look at how you have behaved. You should try to view your behaviour through the other person's eyes. For many of us, that's a tough thing to do.

When you are dealing with relationship problems, it is easy to focus on how you feel. There is a great temptation to respond in the moment, but it is usually better to wait until you get a better sense of detachment – until you are able to view the situation through logic rather than through emotion. This is easier said than done.

## Try to find the cause, don't dwell on the effect

It's upsetting when somebody behaves badly towards you, but the situation will only improve when you understand why they might be behaving that way towards you. This will help you to decide what action you can take to address the cause. As a general rule, the better you know someone the easier it is to understand (or discover) where they might be coming from, what their values are, what stresses them, what drives them.

Sometimes we resent or dislike what we hear from others because there is a grain of truth in it. Be honest with yourself. If what this person says is hurtful but accurate, remember not to shoot the messenger. If you don't like the message but it is valid (for example, they are recommending a change to the way sales operate), you need to separate what is being said from how it is being said. Be sure you are not displacing your anger.

## Decide whether you have to do something about this

Can you put up with the behaviour that is upsetting you? It is important here to reflect on how close your professional relationship has to be, how often you have to meet, the effect of this misfiring relationship on your respective teams, the relative power of your respective departments within the organisation, the status and credibility that each of you have within the organisation, and ultimately, any effect on sales or revenue.

If you decide to do nothing about it, you should stop letting it upset you. Your decision to step back and remain detached is a legitimate decision.

Conversely, if you decide to act, you should have a clear plan of action and a clear understanding of the potential consequences before you do anything. Don't rush in and do or say something you may regret.

In the face of aggressive behaviour, how proud are you of your own behaviour? If your behaviour has escalated the confrontation, you might decide that you are as much to blame as the other person is for any breakdown in the relationship. Admitting your part in the problem might be the first step to a better relationship.

## Seek the views of someone you respect

You may simply want an opinion on the individual or your reaction to their behaviour. Or, you may find it helpful to brainstorm with someone the reasons behind the behaviour. Finally, you might want to hear someone else's opinion about your ideas for action or even what you plan to do. These sorts of opportunities to rehearse your ideas or even role play a conversation are invaluable.

## Address behaviour that upsets you in a one-to-one conversation

Depending on the severity of the situation, you can choose different approaches: you can diffuse the situation with humour if appropriate or you can challenge the tone and content of what you have heard. You know yourself best and you'll know what approach you are most drawn to. Try to do this in a way which is not adversarial or confrontational. For example, rather than telling someone you find something offensive, ask them why they chose those particular words.

If the behaviour you find upsetting happens only in front of other people, it may be being said not for your benefit but for the benefit of others in the room. In this case you need to think about where the self-interest of the other person lies. Is this a power play or a tactic in a bigger game, for example? Operational reasons may lie behind the behaviour. Many organisations are internally highly competitive, especially in areas such as sales. If your department is under-performing, this person may feel this gives them the right to behave in this way towards you. If your team has not delivered successfully to target, you may not want to address the behaviour until you have recovered your performance position, which in turn will increase your power.

You need to be very clear about your exact relationship with this individual because it will inform how you approach them. Also, consider this person's behaviour with other people in the organisation. Is he or she patronising and arrogant with everybody – even people they trust, like and respect? If the answer to these questions is 'yes' then you will be in a stronger position than you might think to challenge the behaviour.

If you believe the cause of this person's behaviour is the stress of their position or the challenge of meeting tough targets, you might decide to cut them some slack; you might even offer some form of help which would in turn build the relationship between you.

## Share the burden

If you decide, either for political reasons or because you have tried and failed to address the problems with the relationship, that your differences are irreconcilable, don't forget you can share the burden. Ask a trusted colleague in your team to take over responsibility for parts of the relationship from you.

# Constantly changing goalposts

*The frustration of constantly changing goalposts within a project run by an external unit is immense. As soon as you think you see a way through to a solution, or a way to get to one of your objectives, the goalposts move and you find yourself having to rethink and replan. The frustration can affect your relationships with your own team and with the external 'owner of the goalposts'.*

## First, think:

- Are you someone who supports this moving project or objective?
- What are your organisation's and your own relationships with the external agency like? Is there a history you need to understand?
- Why do the goalposts move?
- What is the quantifiable impact on you, your team and the wider organisation of constantly changing the objectives or deadlines? How can you minimise the impact?
- Have you dealt with this project owner or group before? What has been your experience to date?
- Can you exert pressure on the external unit from further up your own organisation?
- How exposed are you if this goes wrong?
- When you think about this project, do you have any power or influence over it? If so, where and with whom?

# Ideas for action

## Minimise disruption and maximise success

The twin challenges here are to manage the disruption to your team and organisation so that it is minimised and to collaborate successfully with the external unit to make successful what is a positive initiative.

An important aspect is to understand who owns the project both internally and externally, so that if you try to exert pressure or influence decisions, you do so in the right way and with the right people. The challenge for you is that you are neither the project owner nor the project customer and therefore you are trying to influence without authority. You are unlikely to have power over any of them, but can you influence them?

## Be the positive one

You need to be seen to be somebody offering positive solutions rather than complaining about disruption caused by what is a positive project – or at least one which has support elsewhere internally. Naturally you want to protect your team from disruption and you don't want your team's objectives to be compromised. But this can't be at the expense of the project, so you need to work with the project implementer to make the project happen in the least disruptive way.

## Manage the negative impacts

The other critical aspect is the impact on your team and internal or external customers. Develop a best-case and a worst-case scenario and actionable plans around both. By doing this you have a readily adaptable plan to deal with whatever comes your way.

## Make sure the external unit understands what is important to you

You are entirely right to insist that the external agency understands the impact on your team and customers of changed objectives, specifications, dates, or other moved goalposts.

The external agency must accept that there are key stakeholders whose voices must be heard and respected. You need a relationship with the external project leader which allows both of you to develop a collaborative solution which reflects the interests of all engaged stakeholders. You must be very clear about what are acceptable and what are unacceptable disruptions. You need hard examples of what is unacceptable and specific solutions which allow the project to progress while removing or minimising disruption.

## Awareness is half the solution

By making customers aware of the inevitability of disruption and by identifying the benefits the initiative will bring, you manage their expectations and minimise the risk of complaint or disappointment. By making the external partner aware of the effects of constant changes, especially on your customers or clients, you provide a business-critical context within which the external partner has to work.

## Understand the politics

This sort of challenging partnering with externals is often an aspect of a complex project with multiple stakeholders. You will benefit far more by being collaborative and by being part of a 'best practice' solution than by being seen as an insular manager with a silo mentality. Be aware of the danger of creating or contributing to an 'us and them' relationship between your organisation and the partner external organisation.

Your current role probably doesn't represent the whole of your ambition. Seeing any situation through the eyes of someone in a more senior role, and behaving accordingly, will be seen by others as a sign of maturity and high potential.

# Company merger or acquisition

*Whether you merge, acquire or become acquired, no one can argue that this is one of the most turbulent periods in the life of an organisation. Of the many challenges that managers must face this one is the most all-encompassing. Whether it's the increased internal politics, the fear of the unknown, the need to form relationships or the need to master new systems and processes, there is something here to concern almost anyone. It is the external organisation, the external people and the external partners and suppliers who represent some of the most obvious challenges.*

## First, think:

- Who are the key influencers within your organisation and within the partner organisation? Who have the most influence with external agencies or suppliers?
- Who are the key external agencies working alongside the merging organisations? What will be the nature of your interaction with each of them?
- Is this a hostile takeover or is it something your organisation welcomes?
- How are the members in your team reacting to the plans? What are their worries and concerns?
- How much contact will you need to have with external agencies and/or with the new partner?
- What new skills or competencies do you need to master as a result of this merger or joint venture?

# Ideas for action

## Anticipate emotional fallout

Mergers and acquisitions always involve turmoil; however positive they may be in the long run, there are always people who lose out or who are concerned they might lose out. As a manager, you have an important role to support your people as they undertake this difficult journey. In the face of change, people regularly go through a number of responses. These might include rejecting the change, resisting it, exploring it, and eventually committing to it. Each of your team members will react differently, depending on their personal circumstances and the way in which the change affects them. You will have to deal with an array of emotions, from anger to sadness, from elation to depression, from triumph to a sense of betrayal.

You also need to deal with your own emotional responses to this change. Like your team members, your own responses may swing between positive and negative and you may be surprised by the strength of your own emotional response to the change. Once you understand what your worries are, you can take some practical steps to address those that are under your control. You may find yourself engaging with new or under-developed skills. For example, you could find yourself needing to work with lawyers or accountants, or with consultants in areas such as logistics, pensions or employment law.

## There will be uncertainty everywhere

Remember that the other organisation involved in the merger or joint venture, as well as the many other external agencies, may be feeling as uncertain and as stressed as you and your colleagues. Your ability to come across as considered, balanced and sympathetic will both improve the process and build your reputation.

## This is a good time to be pragmatic

Make a list of the skills you have which you think will be particularly useful during this time. Think about how you can best contribute to the merger and offer your services in this area to the appropriate people. If there are particular areas where you want to exert influence, one of the best things you can do is invest some time in understanding where the two organisations currently stand and where they need to go. For example, in many mergers the merged organisation has more office space and real estate than it needs. Understanding the issues involved in breaking leases or selling freeholds and being willing to get engaged in the complex negotiations that will inevitably happen might give you an opportunity to impress.

### Upskill yourself

Often you will find yourself dealing with external agents who have deep expertise where you have a passing understanding. You need to get the balance right between being led by experts and being vulnerable to the self-interest of other groups. Don't be afraid to keep asking questions to build your own understanding and to make sure that the recommendations being made suit the purposes of your own organisation.

### Build your network

When two organisations get together, networking becomes even more important. You will benefit from having a strong network within your company, but you should also reach out to network with as many people as you can from the company with which you are joining forces, and with the external agencies involved in the merger. This extended network will prove invaluable both when dealing with external agencies and as the newly merged organisation begins to take shape. You never know when a good word from an unexpected source will come in useful.

### Be committed

In these types of situations time is always at a premium and quick decisions are often demanded. You will need to be assertive to make sure that you make informed decisions rather than immediate decisions. This might involve you committing more time than usual to your professional life.

This shouldn't last long but it is probably an investment worth making.

Mergers and acquisitions are somewhat like times of war: in all the hubbub and confusion, there are reputations to be made and opportunities to accelerate career progression.

# 4

# Challenges around conflict

Your job is to be able to recognise whether the conflict you are observing is functional or dysfunctional and then knowing what to do next. This section has practical advice which will help you to resolve conflict where necessary and embrace it where appropriate.

Once you accept that conflict exists whenever people hold different opinions, you quickly realise that conflict is a daily staple of professional life. The question is not whether there is conflict that you'll have to manage; the question is rather how you will manage the conflict that you are bound to encounter. We'll look at what happens when people do try to brush conflict under the carpet, think about how to deal with both emotionless and emotional individuals, consider the challenges of highly competitive behaviour, reflect on situations where everything becomes a win/lose competition, and think about passive-aggressive behaviour.

It's useful to think of conflict as functional or dysfunctional. Functional conflict is healthy, and helps a team or group to meet its objectives; it's the sort of conflict that engenders debate from which spring new ideas, new approaches and new understanding. Dysfunctional conflict hinders the team in its goal of delivering against objectives because it causes people to become distracted and to turn their energy to the conflict rather than to the objectives. This sort of conflict is often competitive, often interpersonal, often rooted in people misunderstanding each other or not respecting the other's preferences or strengths.

# Individuals who avoid conflict

*When you bring initiatives or ideas to people, you might expect a robust debate and exchange of views before any decision. If what you get is evasion and a disinclination to engage in any sort of dialogue, you may get frustrated and lose some confidence, both in yourself and in the person you have approached. Your inability even to get these initiatives discussed may cause you to lose credibility with your team. The root cause is the individual who is conflict averse, avoiding any sort of interaction which might lead to disagreement.*

## First, think:

- What is the decision-making process that the individual seems to favour?
- How do you handle conflict? Are you assertive? Forthright?
- How extreme are the suggestions you are making? Are they suggestions that represent revolution or evolution?
- Is this person well regarded? What is your internal reputation?
- How is the company doing generally? Is this a good time for the sorts of changes you want to champion?
- What is the culture like? Is there a norm for 'how to get things done around here'?
- What have you promised your team around the changes you would like to implement? Is the team supportive of your plans?

# Ideas for action

## Understand the decision-making process

Some companies have a preference for making decisions quickly while others prefer to consult widely; equally, some organisations have clear and transparent decision-making processes while others are more opaque and oblique. Because decision making is so closely associated with handling conflict, it's important that you are very familiar with both the process and the culture around decision making in your organisation.

## Decide whether the initiative is worth it

How strongly do you feel about the initiative? If the suggestion you are making is revolutionary rather than evolutionary, it will be harder to get agreement. The likely attitude and approach of the person whose approval or permission you need will colour your judgement as well. If the individual is conflict averse, making progress will be significantly harder.

## Know whom you need to persuade, and how

It's important to understand the decision maker's preferred approach to handling conflict. If their approach is one of unwillingness to engage in any discussion which might link to conflict, then this determination to avoid conflict means that there is no resolution to the issue and it is therefore a lose–lose situation.

If you are confident that you have support from other key players within the organisation and they share your perception that your targeted decision maker is a conflict-avoider, then you may be able to push harder against any resistance. Equally, if you are the only one who finds that person conflict averse, it may be that it is your personal approach to conflict which provokes this reaction.

## Be honest with yourself about yourself

Self-awareness is particularly important when you are dealing with potential conflict. Be honest with yourself about your style and your own approach to conflict. For example, if you are overtly competitive then this might itself cause the person you need to persuade to want to avoid any situation where there might be conflict with you. Awareness of other people's styles and respect for a diversity of approaches to conflict is also vital. If you constantly approach somebody in a way that they find unsuitable, unattractive or even threatening then you are unlikely to get a very good hearing from them.

This scenario has the potential to be very frustrating, so this is a good opportunity to take advantage of a mentor. You can ask the mentor's advice, but also the very act of sharing your frustration will help you feel better.

## Reflect the company culture

It is important when you bring new ideas or initiatives that you do so in a way that shows an understanding of the culture the organisation has towards discussion and debate, and the processes the organisation has around decision making. For example, some organisations actively encourage an adversarial approach where you are expected to be able to defend robustly your views and recommendations in the face of comment and criticism from others. Other organisations are more formal and hierarchical, requiring written recommendations which are then considered and commented upon. Room for discussion and debate is more limited. Yet other organisations require you to seek consensus through collaborative discussion which consults widely around the organisation. This is a softly-softly approach where influencing is a key factor in any success.

## Make sure you care

You need to be clear on how passionate you are about your ideas. If you feel very strongly, it is easy to come across to others as being stubborn, emotional or even aggressive. When you put new ideas forward you have to think about how others might see them. If they represent evolution – doing things better – then they may well represent less of a threat than if you offer radical ideas which are revolutionary – doing different things. How you present evolution will be different from how you present revolution. People are more likely to respond from their favourite conflict-handling position when faced with revolutionary ideas.

## Understand how the conflict averse might behave

It's often better with conflict-averse people to present them with your ideas in written form and give them time to consider them, rather than make them discuss the ideas with you on the spur of the moment. When you ask a conflict-averse individual to make a decision it is often helpful to include a risk analysis which clearly shows where the risks lie and how they can be modified. This will help give the individual confidence to make a decision.

Another idea is to show what happens if no decision is made and to give a clear timeframe in which a decision needs to be made. All of these things take the uncertainty out of your suggestion, maximising the chances of getting a discussion going with someone who finds conflict difficult to manage. As a further safeguard, if there is somebody whom you know your line manager trusts and respects, try to get this person on board and persuade them to encourage the line manager towards your recommendation.

The challenge of having a conflict-averse decision maker is that it discourages initiatives and innovative thinking. Make sure that what you see as being conflict averse is not seen by the individual concerned as appropriate caution.

## Understand the bigger picture

Contracting economies and organisations under pressure tend to lead to individual decision makers being more conservative or risk averse. Make sure that you understand the bigger picture and present your ideas in that context.

## Engage with your team early

Generally you won't take ideas and initiatives up the organisation without having discussed them with your team. There is a delicate balance here: you need your team's support but you must not over-promise if you know that approval will be difficult to obtain. It's also important, if you don't get the approval you need, that you don't suggest to your team that it's due to any weakness or shortfall on the part of the decision maker.

## Be flexible

The primary trick with a cautious, conflict-averse boss is to emphasise your collaborative nature and downplay your assertiveness or competitiveness. You have to create a situation in which your boss is persuaded rather than coerced into agreement. The best outcome is where your boss feels you and he or she have worked together to create an outcome which is better than the current situation.

# People who don't show emotion

*You may from time to time find a need to interact with a colleague, team member or stakeholder who seems to you always to be withdrawn, insular and incapable of feeling or showing emotion. You may find such an individual difficult, and indeed progress may be hindered by this somewhat distant attitude. Nevertheless, you have to be able to form and maintain a good working relationship.*

## First, think:

- What is your working relationship like with this individual? Do you feel your relationship is or could be complementary? Might others enjoy your very different styles?
- Do you respect what this person brings to joint encounters?
- Is the other person happy with your relationship?
- Do you find it difficult to trust someone whom you don't know well at an individual level?
- Is it really progress that is being hindered or is it your enjoyment of the process?
- Do other people have an issue with what you perceive as this individual's lack of emotion?
- How is the person perceived elsewhere in the organisation?

## Ideas for action

### Value differences in people

While there are types of people to whom we are naturally drawn, it's important that we value what a variety of different types can bring to teams and projects. We can respect and admire an individual's professional contributions without needing to warm to them or be friends with them. Teams need different skills, which are often reflected in different personalities. You need to differentiate between people you like to work with and people whose work you like.

## Be pro-active

It is vital to accept different behaviours and styles, even if they are not to your personal taste. However, you have to take some action when management styles start to impact team performance or morale. Your options are to address the issue with the individual, with the individual's boss or with your boss. If you have already tried to address the issue with the individual and you have been rebuffed, it is still worth trying again before you elevate the situation to the next level of management. Elevating situations will almost always exacerbate behaviour, causing the individual to become more defensive, more insular or more passive-aggressive.

## Talk to the person

This will be a difficult conversation and a good manager will do everything possible to mitigate the difficulty by both preparing for the conversation thoroughly and presenting the problem as reasonably as possible. Something that's easily forgotten in these difficult conversations is the importance of not patronising and not bullying the other person.

You should not dwell on the past but instead focus on the changes needed to restore energy and momentum to the relationship. Be sure that you acknowledge the strengths that the individual brings to the team or to the team's activities. The outcome has to be that together you agree a way of working that is best for the team and for success.

Part of your preparation for this meeting will be to take soundings from project team members, colleagues and stakeholders. You will need to be sensitive, adept and adroit when you do this. The key is in the choice of questions you ask. It's important not to discredit or undermine the other person's reputation or position. Asking questions of others about performance and progress, strengths and challenges, enthusiasm and commitment to deliver will all help to reveal frustration (if any) with the individual's style.

## It isn't all about you

Bear in mind that the objective of this project is not necessarily for you to be personally more content. Projects or tasks that require interdependent action take on their own personalities; the dynamics of each situation will change depending on the individuals involved. Take a step back: be sure it's not your need to be enjoying the process or to have control that is making you uncomfortable with this individual's personal dynamic.

Something you might consider is to let another team member whose personality might better gel with this particular person take a more prominent role in those activities where the individual is involved and/or important.

## Evaluate and understand the risk

It is certainly the case that work which requires interdependent action for success is more likely to meet with that success if stakeholders are able to engage not only with their own team but also with other involved individuals. So the insular individual who may prefer introvert behaviours equally has a responsibility to do what is necessary to build relationships with other key stakeholders and between his or her team and other engaged teams.

It's useful to think more broadly than about just the performance metrics of the project; a project can be going well but if morale is in decline, this must be addressed or the project progress will eventually suffer. If this individual is part of a long-term or complex project, you may look to invest in team-building activities which seek to build individual connections and help individuals appreciate and build upon the diversity within the project team.

# Emotional people

*Inevitably work can sometimes become an emotional place. However, you may find an individual team member is too frequently finding it difficult to manage his or her emotions. Perhaps it is when anyone tries to disagree, critique output or offer an alternative point of view that this individual becomes disproportionately upset or defensive even to the point of welling up in tears. The emerging issue may be that people will become increasingly unwilling to engage in conflict with this person, which is affecting the efficiency of the team.*

## First, think:

- How long has this behaviour been going on? Should you have addressed this situation earlier? Has anyone inside or outside the team complained about the behaviour?
- What are you noticing with regard to loss of efficiency and quality? How significant is the impact of the behaviour on the team?
- Where is the individual in the pecking order of the team? Is the person well liked and well regarded?
- Is this behaviour restricted to within the team or does this person behave this way with clients, customers or other departments?
- How have others tried to deal with these outbursts in the past?
- How comfortable are you in dealing with emotional responses to professional challenges?
- What are the behavioural styles of the other members of the team? Is this emotional style an exception within the team?

# Ideas for action

## Understand the context before addressing the problem

The more you know, the more you understand, the better your chances of having constructive conversations with this emotional person. So, find out as much as you can about the individual and their history within the organisation and elsewhere. Is this a recurring issue or a new development? If there is any knowledge of their circumstances away from work, try to access that knowledge. Take discreet soundings from other stakeholders about the individual.

Try hard to form a personal relationship with the person, not a friendship necessarily, but at a minimum a good professional relationship which goes beyond the normal manager–team member level.

All the time you are looking for something that has changed in the individual's circumstances to which they may have responded badly. This could be a promotion (they feel they can't cope, perhaps) or being passed over for a role (they may feel unvalued or betrayed). It may be that someone has joined or left the team and affected the interpersonal relationships in a way that has upset this individual. Someone may be coercing the individual or making them collude in something about which they are uneasy or unhappy.

## Deal with the cause of the problem, not the effect

You can't just deal with the individual's tendency towards overt emotion. You need to understand and address what is igniting that tendency. It may be work related, such as career frustration, the stress associated with a challenging job or a sense of being undervalued, for example. But it may just as likely be something away from work – a troubled relationship, a family or personal illness, money problems or any one of many other potential challenges. If all you do is challenge the behaviour and not the cause of the behaviour, you are unlikely to find a sustainable resolution.

## Address any team performance issues with the team as well as the individual

If the individual's rather too emotional responses are resulting in others avoiding offering challenges or creating constructive discontent, then you do have to address this. Make sure the team knows you are aware of and are addressing the issue. Ask for patience and understanding. Make sure the individual understands that while you intend to work to address the cause of this behaviour, you do need the person to try hard to manage the behaviour so that it stops holding back the team. Both these conversations are critical and potentially difficult and you will need to know your team and the particular individual well before embarking on them.

## Review your own behaviour

If you feel on reflection that you should have done more, sooner, you should admit that to the individual. If you have failed to offer this person the support they need and want, then you too are part of the problem. If emotional responses at work is an area where you are uneasy or unsympathetic, you need to get out of your comfort zone and stretch yourself to address this challenge. Be absolutely sure that you know your own team members well enough.

# Competitive behaviour

*Often organisations thrive on high levels of internal competition; in many, performance is measured and performance tables are regularly published. Some individuals always want to top the performance tables. This can lead to displays of highly competitive behaviour. If people are taking competitiveness to an extreme, the impact on team culture, morale and performance may be significant, creating a circumstance where it is competitiveness itself which brings down the team.*

## First, think:

- Do you know what is likely to happen when this highly competitive person appears to want to compete with you and others?

- Do you genuinely believe that there is a better way than to be competitive? Or are you concerned that you cannot compete effectively?

- What is your history with your colleague? Have you worked together much in the past? Do you like the person at an individual level?

- What is the rewarded behaviour within your team and organisation? What are the noticeable impacts on the team and on individuals within it of this person's competitive approach to conflict?

- How can you bring about a change in behaviour without imposing it – and what if you try to do that and fail?

# Ideas for action

## Make sure everyone knows when it's OK to compete

Successful individuals have a clear understanding of their own approach to internal competitiveness and its impact on career advancement. People who would not compete with a client are often perfectly happy to compete with colleagues, particularly if they see their own ambitions under threat. You need to be sure that your team members understand exactly how you feel about win–lose versus win–win behaviour.

## Collaboration must be valued internally

You must both support and model collaborative behaviour if you want others to behave in that way. It must be understood to be an important part of the team culture which everyone agrees is necessary for team success. If you do that, then competitive behaviour can be challenged as counter-cultural.

If you can have an honest conversation with this particularly competitive colleague to agree a way to behave which is mutually beneficial, then you have succeeded in creating a collaborative solution. Be prepared, though, for resistance and refusal. Highly assertive individuals do not find it easy to agree such a course of action.

## Be ready to compete if necessary

Because competitive people can force you into a competitive position (it's hard to do anything but compete sometimes) you do need to be clear about how competitive you can be. Do a SWOT analysis on yourself and your colleague, being honest about each area. When you look at the result, the question you need to ask yourself is: if I compete, how likely am I to win? Before you make your decision you should consider whether you can 'up your game' in areas where your colleague is particularly strong. This may require you to accept that you need to become better at things you don't much like doing.

There is something honest about overt competitive behaviour: the ambition is at least naked. Often people are less honestly competitive, engaging instead in subversive or manipulative competitive behaviour. You need to be sure you are not one of these people, criticising an overtly competitive colleague when you are yourself covertly competitive. If you have to be competitive, the trick is to compete on your terms, using your strengths. Once you have really analysed your strengths, play to them.

A significant danger here is that this battle of ambition will result in the team being poorly served. If the battle is so public and obvious as to draw the attention of others outside the team, then the reputation of the entire team could suffer.

## Culture is more important than approaches to conflict

You may choose not to take the head-on competitive approach with this colleague. Step back and take a look at the long-term game. It may be that this colleague's competitiveness causes irritation or even anger among stakeholders. Your colleague's competitiveness may gain a short-term advantage over you, but in the long term such an approach may well become self-destructive. This is because extremely competitive people are uncooperative and eventually enough stakeholders will notice this or suffer from it, causing that competitive attitude to be challenged.

A constant challenge for ambitious people is balancing their personal ambition with the political ramifications of each decision they make. Nobody wants to be seen as a destroyer of team or organisational cultures, but that is just what competitive people do within a predominantly collaborative culture. The role of the manager is to contextualise competitive behaviour: make it clear when and where it has a role and when and where it has no role.

## You may have to compete about the competitive behaviour

You can't collaborate with somebody who is determined to compete with you. Your only choice is to accommodate them or to compete with them. If you choose to compete, you will have to be extremely assertive in the face of their well-honed, competitive behaviour, and you will need to accept that the message to the rest of the team is 'forget collaboration, let's all be competitive with each other!'.

Often an appropriate time to be competitive might be when you have the necessary constructively critical conversation with your colleague. You may start by trying to find a win–win solution, only to be met with more competitive behaviour. You really cannot afford to avoid this or to give in: you simply have to win, if necessary by using your authority to impose strictures around behaviour on your colleague. You will want to be well prepared for this meeting and armed with a steely determination.

# Passive-aggressive behaviour

*Sometimes colleagues may appear to agree with a manager and accept a course of action but then do nothing to put that agreed course of action in place. This affects the performance of the team, because things remain undone, and disagreement is better discussed and resolved rather than treated in this way. However, whenever this behaviour is challenged, the individual simply does the same thing: agrees with the criticism and accepts the need to change, but does not then make any change.*

## First, think:

- Can this person do what they have agreed to do? If so, why, in your view, does it remain undone? Is this unwillingness recent? Does it relate to some tasks or all tasks?
- When you think about the things this colleague agrees to do but then does not, are these things that have been delegated or are they part of the individual's own role? Does anyone have the authority to ask this person to undertake these tasks?
- Is your relationship with this person becoming more fraught because of the passive-aggressive behaviour?
- What is your colleague's professional reputation within the organisation? Is this behaviour displayed with other people?
- How would you describe yourself? Are you forthright? Would you describe yourself as orientated more towards people, tasks or analysis?
- How does your colleague's behaviour affect the team's performance? How many other stakeholders are affected by this behaviour and its outcome?

# Ideas for action

## Discover the cause of the behaviour

The important thing to understand in this situation is what exactly is driving this individual's behaviour. Is it anger? Is it stubbornness? Is it a lack of listening? Or is it even competitive behaviour? You need to deal with the root cause of the conflict – not the behaviour that you are experiencing.

A particular challenge around passive-aggressive behaviour is the amount of energy-sapping frustration it creates. This frustration affects not just you but also the people who have to experience the effects of things not being done. A further aspect of this frustration is that whatever you do, nothing appears to change, and in the end you lose all trust that a passive-aggressive individual will do anything they undertake and agree to do.

## Commit to that difficult conversation

To get to the root cause requires you to be able to have a deep and possibly personal conversation with this individual. If your relationship with this colleague goes beyond the surface, you can leverage this to encourage a deeper level of discussion. In moments of candour and openness and in an informal setting, you may discover why this individual is prepared to commit with no intention of delivering. Don't underestimate the difficulty of this. Many people who are passive-aggressive won't share the root cause of their behaviour; indeed, they may not even be aware of the cause(s) themselves.

Generally the way to deal with unwillingness is to form a coaching relationship with the individual which tries to get to the bottom of why the individual is unwilling. Reasons may include lack of confidence, resentment and lack of self-esteem.

## Attempt immediately to address the effects of the behaviour

Regardless of whether you can get to the root cause, you do need to deal with the effects, especially if they are having an impact on performance. You may need to use the power of your authority to impose a change in behaviour while you deal separately with seeking the cause of the behaviour. What you probably can't afford to do is allow the negative impact of the behaviour to continue unchecked while you work with the individual towards identifying the cause.

## You'll need a process to manage the behavioural change

At the heart of passive-aggressive behaviour is an undertaking to do something which you will not then go on to do. It is a lack of willingness rather than a lack of ability. So, it is important that all agreed actions are carefully noted and, in particular, that the fact of agreement to act is noted. This means that the passive-aggressive individual has a commitment to deliver which might encourage them when their unwillingness begins to take hold.

## Learn from others

You should spend time finding out what other people think of this colleague. Do they share your experiences? If they do and they have resolved their frustrations, you can learn from them. If they continue to be frustrated, at a minimum you can gain some comfort from knowing that you are not alone in experiencing difficulties. Together you may be able to think of a way to deal with the problem.

## Is it you?

If you discover that you alone have this issue, it may be that the passive-aggressive response has, at its root, the nature and quality of your personal relationship with this colleague. You now know what you need to examine: what you are asking of this individual and how you are demanding it. The question you are seeking to answer is why is it only you who evokes this response?

Maybe you are micro-managing this person. A common stimulus for passive-aggressive behaviour is not just asking a colleague to do something but telling that colleague exactly how to do it. The colleague, feeling bruised and used as a resource, will agree to do it but has no intention of delivering. Make sure that when you ask anyone to do anything, you leave them appropriate room to decide how to do it.

If you are asking your colleague to do things which that individual may feel are inappropriate or beneath them, and they feel they cannot argue with, then that person may well use passive-aggressive behaviour. Equally, if the division of labour is sound but the style that you use is clumsy or demeaning, then you may get this passive-aggressive response.

## Or is it them?

Passive-aggressive people are generally conflict averse. This may be because they are lacking in assertion and/or confidence. You can and should encourage people to understand that it's OK to say no if they think they are being asked to do things they don't agree with, but it isn't OK to agree to do something and then not deliver.

# 5

Challenges around change

You'll find a world of opportunity in change: successful change implementers and change champions are highly valued in organisations. But equally with change initiatives comes risk – and especially the risk of the change failing. This section will help you to maximise your contribution to successful change making.

We are frequently told that change is the only constant in today's business environment. So, it makes sense for organisations to expect managers like you to be adept at helping to make change happen and at helping people through change. Many managers find enough trouble with this when the people under their management want to embrace the change. But how often is it really the case that change is warmly embraced and universally welcomed within the organisation? Many change initiatives have as many losers as winners, and a constant diet of change can weary even the most enthusiastic appetite.

Change can fail for many reasons. But one of the most common is a refusal among those affected to accept it. In more straitened economies, where much change is about contraction rather than expansion, and about getting more for less and from fewer people, it is even less surprising that change can be challenging.

This section of the book helps you to recognise how different people can react differently to the demands of change. It helps you to understand how better to help people – whether their resistance is covert or overt, whether they deny the necessity of change or simply resist it and refuse to explore the possibilities and opportunities the change represents. We'll talk too about dealing with people who have become too comfortable to contemplate change. Of course, it isn't all bad: some teams really do have a genuine taste for change, and we'll help you to understand how best to maintain such a team's high-energy change culture.

# Covert resistance to change

*As tricky as it can be for managers to tempt individuals to accept and embrace change, it is far more difficult if there is an individual who says they are on board but is secretly undermining your change efforts. If you suspect that an individual in the team, while not openly opposing the change to you, is presenting a negative interpretation to colleagues, you may have good cause for concern. The individual may sway opinion and generate some support, causing the change initiative to wobble or even to fall over entirely.*

## First, think:

- What makes you feel you are being covertly opposed? What has aroused your suspicion?
- Is this person's behaviour typical in the face of change? Does this change have a particular personal or professional impact on this person? Is there a possibility this is personal to you rather than about the change initiative?
- What is your relationship like with other individuals within the team and with this person in particular? Is the team culture generally open and supportive or are there some hidden agendas?
- Does this person represent a scarce skill or is he or she replaceable?
- Can the change successfully be opposed or prevented?
- How are you perceived as a manager within the organisation? Do you have a strong reputation?
- What is your response to the change? Do you stand to gain from it professionally? Do you feel insecure about the coming change?

# Ideas for action

### Learn to spot covert resistance

Covert resistance is often subtle and difficult to spot and therefore hard to confront. It's at the tricky times that you get payback for your past commitment to building an open and communicative team where people are encouraged to voice their opinions, including opinions opposing those of management.

### Gather evidence first

You have to be sure of your ground before you attempt to confront covert opposition. Remember, you need some sort of clear evidence, as denial is the most likely form of defence that the covert operator will offer. Covert opposition is an act of 'internal terrorism' and, like all terrorism, is extraordinarily difficult to oppose. Your covert terrorist requires the support of at least some of the rest of the team. Your best hope is to rely on the quality of the relationship you have built with your team. This, combined with the culture you have created, which should be one of transparency and mutual support, should allow you to find out from team members whether there is covert opposition.

### Understand your team and the relationships within it

Critical to dealing with this dilemma successfully is an absolutely thorough understanding of how your team works. You need to be sure of the prevailing culture in your team, and you need to have a clear sense both of how individuals behave and of how they really feel about this change.

The next thing to do is consider very carefully your relationship with the individual you suspect. If the person has a history of covert actions or if you feel the person has a particularly poor opinion of or relationship with you, then it is more likely your suspicions are well founded. You might also consider what the individual has to lose if the change initiative goes ahead, and also what might be gained by usurping your authority.

The moment you try to validate your suspicions by approaching the person you suspect or other team members, you escalate the issue. You should be very wary of doing this unless you are convinced that your suspicions are well founded.

You also need to reflect on how you see yourself. If you are new to management, have low self-esteem or are too anxious about being liked, you must consider the possibility that your suspicions say more about you than about the team or the individual. Equally, if you stand to gain a lot from this change initiative, you should be cautious about seeing covert resistance where none in fact exists.

## Consider your approach options carefully

If, after reflecting on all of the above, you remain convinced that an issue exists, approach the individual about whom you have suspicions. The likely outcome is that of denying any involvement. However, if you feel you have established a transparent and open culture within your team and you would like to continue to role-model those behaviours, you may feel this is the most appropriate first step.

An alternative or a next step is to approach other members of the team. How you approach individuals is just as important as who you approach. The tone of your conversation with individuals must be non-accusatory and subtle. Without concrete evidence, it is important not to alienate any members of your team. Remember, it is generally difficult for team members to blow the whistle on colleagues, particularly if they feel the colleague's point of view has some merit.

If you are relatively new to this team then you will find this naturally more difficult. Nevertheless, because you cannot avoid this challenge, you will have to rely on your early impressions and talk with the individuals with whom you have developed good early connections. If, during this process, you do establish to your own satisfaction that the individual you suspect is covertly recruiting other team members, then your first step is to obtain permission from the whistle-blowers to use their input as evidence with which to challenge the individual. Ideally, you also want their overt support to discussing the issue as a team.

## Decide what is acceptable to you as a solution

Your ultimate objective is to isolate the disaffected individual so that other team members cannot be recruited to the cause. Your colleague is then left with a stark choice: to fall in line or to continue to be isolated. To achieve this, given that you want to avoid a hurtful confrontation, you must ask for a further public commitment from every member of the team to the impending change. Your disaffected team member will either offer public support or not. Either way, their credibility is seriously undermined.

If the dissenting individual in your team has a scarce skill and is therefore of particular value to the team, their acceptance of the change initiative becomes disproportionately important. You might decide to recruit other stakeholders whom this individual respects, whose job would be to persuade your colleague of the need to support the change initiative.

If you're confident this change can be neither prevented nor derailed and that your team believe this as well, then you may decide to trust to the good judgement of your team to manage the covert dissatisfaction themselves. You might decide that as the individual is guaranteed to fail, it is better for you to allow that failure than to try to prevent the attempt.

## Avoid further problems

This type of covert behaviour can spread like slow poison, which can be very damaging to the team's culture and performance. If you cannot put a stop to the divisive behaviour, you may be left with no option but to ask the individual to leave the organisation.

# Overt resistance to change

*Change is a constant in the modern working world. You can't allow individuals to hold change back through resistance. It might be possible to be flexible, but sometimes it simply isn't. Part of your job is to help manage people through the constant change processes which exist. But what do you do when you encounter a real 'heels dug in' attitude to change?*

## First, think:

- What is this person's contribution to the team? What value do they bring?
- Is there justification to the opposition? Does your colleague offer alternatives to the opposed change? Is this aversion to change affecting the quality of work presented?
- How have you dealt with this resistance in the past? Have you always given in?
- What is the impact of these changes on this individual? Does it involve a loss of influence, authority or position for your colleague?
- How vocal and how influential is this individual? Is there any attempt to gather support among the rest of the team or among key stakeholders for the view this person holds? How much damage could continued resistance do to the team or to your reputation?
- How committed are you as a manager to helping your colleague deal with this change challenge? What is your personal view of the changes you are having to impose?

# Ideas for action

## Managing resistance is a requirement and not an option

It has been true for many businesses over many years that change is the only constant. The pace of change, however, has accelerated and continues to accelerate. Technology plays a large part in this acceleration but so do the twists and turns of the economy. So, whatever the cause of change, what we do know is that every manager in every organisation has to be adept at managing change. This means helping individuals within their team to understand the need for change and to be prepared to accept the reality of change.

Managers regularly find themselves implementing change that they themselves don't support; indeed they may even themselves be adversely affected. None of this should affect their ability to implement the change and to manage the team through to commitment to the change.

## You are your team's change guide

In this scenario the manager's responsibility is clearly to shepherd the reluctant individual through the change process. This will take time and effort and even then may not make the individual more amenable to future change. However, the manager who does not take on this responsibility ends up managing a change-averse team in a change-rich environment.

Remember that when change is around you are first and foremost the manager implementing the change. If you begin to challenge it in front of the team or if you are too sympathetic to challenges they make, you undermine the change initiative and become part of the change problem rather than the change solution. If you are adamantly opposed to a change, you can challenge up the organisation privately but your public stance must be consistent and positive.

The fine line that every manager must walk is that of committing enough time to those who need attention while also focusing on the balance of the team who are performing well but who still deserve encouragement and praise. This is the squeaky wheel dilemma: how do you decide how much time to spend on the problem and how much time on the opportunity?

## Flexibility is good

Because change can be challenging, the first thing to understand is what, if any, flexibility you have around the implementation of this change. If you can change any part of it to suit the demands of your team, you may find that the change is more readily accepted. Change which is imposed, inflexible and evokes an emotional reaction is the sort of change which is most likely to be resented and resisted.

## Make sure you know the details and ramifications of the change initiative

Your team will expect you to be their primary source of information and will be asking you a lot of detailed questions. This is likely to be especially true of people who are cautious of change.

Be sure, too, that you understand what help you might expect from within the organisation before you announce the change within your team. For example, with major change initiatives there may be a change champion or team of people whose responsibility it is to help you initiate the change. There may also be material created to help people understand the change, the need for it and the benefits of adopting it. All of this can help you to help your team and individuals within it to accept the inevitable.

## There is a pattern to individual reactions to change

It's helpful for managers to understand a typical cycle which individuals may go through when experiencing significant change. The process is similar to the grieving process: first we deny that anything has happened; then we resist the new state of affairs; next we explore the new circumstance; and finally we accept and commit to the new reality. Different people spend different amounts of time in each of the four parts of the cycle. Sometimes people get stuck in a particular place. Your role as manager is to help people understand the cycle and move through it as smoothly and as calmly as possible.

When an individual in your team gets stuck in one of the phases of the cycle – and this individual may be stuck in denial or resistance – then you have to commit the necessary time, energy and effort to help the individual move on towards commitment. Different people need different sorts of help: some want to understand every detail of the change (and its impact on them); others want to explore the need for the change; still others need to understand the vision for the future and need help letting go of the past.

## Different people need different sorts of help

It's important to give people the sort of help they need, but you must also help them to accept that the train is leaving and they've got to get on board or be left behind. How you deal with individuals who are resisting change to some extent depends on their role in the team and their importance to the team. If they have a scarce skill and it is imperative that the team moves forward with them on board then, especially if they realise their own importance, you will need to commit whatever time is necessary to influencing and persuading them.

If such people are also key influencers within the team then their ability to generate a barrier to change is even greater. Another way to help them through the change curve might be to encourage other stakeholders to spend time with them listening to their concerns and, where possible, offering reassurance. Think back to other occasions when such people have been change averse. What has worked in the past? What have they found persuasive and compelling? The same techniques may work in this circumstance. They are at least worth trying.

You should know your team members well enough to know what motivates or incentivises them, just as you should know what concerns or upsets them. You may be able to use this knowledge to choose the most compellingly effective influencing approach with those who are averse to the change. Perhaps others will be able to help you based on their knowledge and understanding of these employees.

## Big changes generate big reactions

The bigger and more emotional the change, the chances are the bigger and more emotional the response. Particularly when dealing with employees who are change averse, it is imperative that you think through and plan how you will approach their reticence. Your first chance is by far your best chance. If you try and fail, it is likely that they will become even more entrenched in their resistance.

The skill of a good manager is to be able to paint a vision of the future with the change in place which is attractive and achievable for the team and the individuals within it.

# Denial

*People's reactions to change will differ depending upon their personality, their historical experiences of change initiatives and the potential impact of the change initiative on them. Sometimes an employee reacts to impending change with denial, refusing to acknowledge the benefits of the change. If you are concerned that time has not helped that person move forward and that they may become a stumbling block to the successful implementation of the change plans, you must take action.*

## First, think:

- Have you listened to his or her concerns? Are they presented in a balanced way? Does he or she always seek to maintain the status quo?

- What does this individual have to lose when the change initiative is implemented? What do the other team members think of this change? How much input did this person and your team have in this change process?

- Is this change an externally generated change imposed on the team or an internally generated change that the team has sought?

- If the change initiative involves requiring new skills from team members, what additional training will be provided?

- What is your relationship with this individual? Is it generally positive and mutually respectful? What is his or her relationship with the other team members?

# Ideas for action

## Honour the past

As the team's manager it is important that you honour the past as much as you look forward to an invigorating new future. You need to remember how much time, energy and effort has been invested in the status quo; people may feel that respect has not been given to how things were done in the past and that you are now carelessly discarding their hard work.

## Understand the change to be made

If well-established systems or procedures are going to change, you need to acknowledge that knowledge and understanding of those systems or procedures may represent a power base for the people in your department. If the individual who is in denial understands those systems better than anyone else, then you are removing the source of that power.

It's worth remembering that the easiest change to implement is that which the team members themselves identify as necessary. Once the team accepts that some change is necessary then you can engage them in deciding exactly what has to change and how.

## People can find change overwhelming

This tricky situation may also be caused because the individual concerned is simply overwhelmed at the prospect of this change or may be fearful about losing his or her job or status in the organisation. Some people find change more difficult than others, and if the change undermines their competence and therefore threatens their power, they are likely to become shocked and angry, denying that the change is necessary. Something that exacerbates this is the thought that the change has been imposed rather than chosen. Imposed change can make people feel redundant or victimised. Change that the team chooses for themselves is change they are far more likely to accept.

You must spend time with this individual, discussing the change in the context of competition, market or industry trends. Persuading them out of denial requires you to offer up both a fact-based rationale and a vision-based story of the future. It is particularly important to communicate the purpose and benefits of the change and explain the benefits for them. For example, if there are customer-related benefits to the change, such as simpler invoices, more accurate invoicing or quicker invoicing times, emphasise these benefits to the team. They may find it helpful to talk to other people who have been through a similar change process.

Two other things are important. The first is that you do not get emotional with reluctant employees. The other is that you do not back off: the change is inevitable, so not addressing the issue is not an option.

You should respect the experience the change-averse individual brings and ask them to articulate why they are so opposed to the change. They may have a view which is valid and a useful contribution to make, particularly given their expertise and length of service.

## It's frustrating when inevitable change is opposed

But you must be patient: people have a right to resist and to come to terms with change in their own time and in their own way. If you are impatient you will simply prolong the resistance. You have to listen, empathise and offer support. As soon as you hear anything that sounds like the beginnings of acceptance, you should offer lots of praise and encouragement. All of this will take time and you should be prepared to invest time in managing the response of individuals to the change. The quality of your communication is important. You have to make sure the team knows exactly what is going to happen and when.

You also need to make sure they are completely aware of the training and support programmes that will be on offer during the change process. These are important aspects of reassurance which will help people to manage the legitimate concerns they may have about the effects of the change on how they work.

Ask someone in the team who finds the change exciting and positive to help your reluctant team members to come to terms with what is going to happen.

## Helping people cope with change is a challenge every manager faces

The manager who can successfully guide individuals successfully through change is one who will be highly valued by their team and their organisation.

# People who are too comfortable

*When you manage a team which has achieved consistent success over several years, success can become a way of life. Keeping people motivated, challenged and driving forward may become a concern. A sign of a team that is becoming too comfortable is when they focus internally on aspects which have more to do with process and environment than with their customer-facing responsibilities. It is important to maintain drive and momentum, because a culture of comfort is not sustainable and can leave you vulnerable to both external competitive activity and internal dissatisfaction.*

## First, think:

- What are the specific signs of contentment that you have picked up? Is your view shared by others?
- What have you already done to try to re-energise the team? How is your team perceived internally and externally by others? Are they meeting performance levels and service-level agreement targets?
- Can you trace the inertia you see emerging within the team to an individual or to a number of individuals? Or is it wholesale?
- How does this team culture of 'contentment' compare to other teams within the organisation? Do you see ways to increase the levels of challenge?
- Is it possible that you too are losing your sharpness and appetite?

- If you fear external activity, what is different about the competitor's circumstances compared to your own? What is happening in the industry?

# Ideas for action

## Understand each individual within your team intimately

Even when a team is on cruise control, it is rare that each individual within a team is happy with being comfortable and unchallenged. The better you know each of your team members, the better you can identify those who really would like things to be more challenging, more exciting, more volatile. These are the team members most likely to support you when you try to generate excitement, passion and commitment around doing things in a different way, or around doing different things. These individuals are likely to be the people in the team who are still ambitious, both for themselves and for the team itself.

Equally, there will be people in the team who are very keen to maintain the comfortable *status quo*. These individuals may be content with what the team has achieved, and prefer a working life which is reasonably predictable and undemanding. These are the people who are likely to resist efforts to reinvigorate the team.

Without appearing to attempt to divide and rule, you should make time to spend with individuals from both these factions, so that before you begin to decide how to re-stimulate the team, you have a very clear idea of where support and resistance are likely to be found and where each might manifest itself.

If you believe that the descent into comfort is primarily driven by one or two team members, think about having critical conversations with them, individually and together, so that you deal with the problem by changing the attitudes and approaches of the people who are responsible for the cosy culture the team is developing.

## Understand the past and present to plan for the future

If you have made previous attempts to galvanise the team, be honest with yourself about why these initiatives have failed, and also make sure you ask individuals in the team why they think the initiatives failed.

Look around at the rest of the organisation. If this is an endemic issue then you may well be better raising it as an organisational issue in management meetings rather than trying to deal with your team alone. If your team is the exception, then you will want to move fast before what is obvious to you becomes apparent to all.

If your organisation does have a history of striving and then resting on a plateau, find out what in the past has re-energised the entire organisation. Perhaps something similar could work again.

## Challenge yourself

Ask yourself whether you are still the best person to lead this team. If the best way to restore the team's energy is to have a new team leader, you will need to acknowledge this. Either seek to step into another role in the organisation, creating a vacancy within your own team, or reinvent yourself so that it feels to the team as if they have a new leader. Look at every-thing you do and ask yourself how you can do it differently, better, in a more involving way.

## Seek alternative views and opinions

Your view of your team is patently important. But it is only one view, and it is the view of someone who is, or should be, very close to the team. So, look for some more objective opinions. Speak to your peers, maybe to your mentor and if appropriate to clients, customers or other stakeholders. Without neces-sarily revealing that you have concerns, elicit their views on the team and on key individuals within it.

Overall, make sure before you make your move that you are as well informed and as well supported as you can be, so that the move you make is most likely to succeed.

## Do something – because doing nothing is not an option

The temptation is to 'wait and see', especially if the team is meeting objectives and the deliverables look to be in good shape. But every aspect of the workplace today is increasingly competitive, and the moment a team is seen by others, internally or externally, to be relaxing, or worse to be stagnating, then change will very quickly be imposed from outside and you will find your team challenged to improve, or be reduced in size, or even disbanded altogether or merged into another unit.

So, the time to deal with people and teams who have become too comfortable is as soon as you see it, not as soon as others do.

# Maintaining the team's high-energy change culture

*When members of the team are young, enthusiastic and ambitious, they often work long hours to ensure work is delivered to the highest standard. They socialise with one another and their professional lives are the centre of their world. But this level of immersion is not sustainable and potential burnout can spell ruin for the team and for the changes the team has embraced.*

## First, think:

- What is the level of energy you feel is ideal for the team? Is that level sustainable and attainable?
- What are the factors that have made the team into a high-performing team? Do you know what motivates each person in the team? What do you identify to be the culture the team has created for themselves?
- Are you driven in the same way as your team?
- Does your team share your concern about their working practices and about potential burnout? How readily could each individual be replaced if there is burnout?
- Do you think the team can deliver to the same standard but with shorter hours?
- Do you have a vision of how you want this team to behave? Have you benchmarked against competitors? What do you definitely not want to change or lose with this team?

# Ideas for action

## Anticipate problems and plan for them

It's great that not only do you have a high-energy, high-performing team but you are also anticipating future potential problems. You have already realised that pre-emptive reflection and action is better than post-emptive reaction and correction.

It is important that you know each individual in your team well enough to know what drives them and what causes them stress. With this knowledge you will be able to provide just enough challenge for each person to keep them energised and positive but not so much that it causes the team to overheat.

The risk is that the team becomes an exclusive club where the entry requirements might include being young and unattached, for example. Team members may be able to offer this level of commitment, but as soon as their circumstances change they will want to reduce their involvement.

## Use their energy to explore ways of working

This is a passionate and engaged team. If you have an open relationship with them, they will readily share with you what they see as fundamental to their current success and how to maintain that success into the future.

## Renew, refresh, rotate and reward

The key for a team to stay in this 'renewal' mode is continually to refresh your team using external benchmarking, job rotation and access to development programmes. Bringing in an outsider will often refresh a well-established team. The outsider might bring new expertise or understanding, or might simply supply more of the skills the team already has. Either way, a new face, new ideas and new relationships can all invigorate a team.

Any team which is constantly managing change and pushing boundaries will, from time to time, fail or at least fail to reach the high standards they have set for themselves. Don't punish this sort of failure or the risk-taking associated with it; it is an inevitable part of managing boundary-pushing change.

Equally, celebrate success. There is a lot of research to suggest that people leave organisations if they are not being recognised and rewarded for the successes to which they contribute. The rewards can be as varied as bonus payments, a celebratory meal together or a genuine and heartfelt thank you.

## Model appropriate and sustainable behaviour

Make it clear that you don't expect people to stay long into the evening and you won't reward them for doing so. There will be exceptions, of course, but the established culture should be that people work reasonable hours. With some individuals you may need to have a conversation in which you are transparent about your concerns regarding their long working hours. While acknowledging how hard they are working, you should help them to see that what they are doing is unsustainable and could lead to them burning themselves out in the future.

If you can establish that team performance is not directly linked to hours spent at work and if you can show that your team's high bar is not affected by working more reasonable hours, then you are setting a powerful example to the rest of the organisation as well as building your own credibility as a successful manager. Pay specific attention to the culture in the team and in the organisation: is macho behaviour (regardless of gender) expected and rewarded? Macho behaviour such as competitive, aggressive high spirits, cruel humour or bawdiness needs to be recognised and acknowledged to be counter-cultural.

The manager's role with a team like this is to harness the energy and the enthusiasm, making sure it is put to best use, and making sure that the energy source is sustainable. If the manager's approach is too hands-off, the team may run out of control, burning their energy too intensely and too quickly.

# 6

Challenges around power, politics and influence

This section offers a grounding to help you to see the connections between power, influence and politics. You'll see how looking at events through the lens of another person's self-interest can often help you to see what political agendas may be active; and you'll see why having your own personal brand – standing for something within the organisation – can help to define you and help to influence the picture others form of you.

In organisational life, everything is political. This is because there is always some combination of open and hidden organisational agendas alongside open and hidden personal agendas. These agendas are often selfish rather than selfless, with individuals pursuing an agenda which favours them or their team or department rather than one which selflessly favours the organisation or the organisation's clients and customers.

You won't be able to create a working culture which removes hidden agendas, so the politics of organisational life will always be with you. The question becomes not 'should I play?' but 'How should I play?'. One can become involved in organisational politics in a way which is appropriate, fair and useful.

After all, being an organisational hermit isn't actually an option for any ambitious manager. It is obviously possible in theory to abstain from the political machinations within an organisation, but your effectiveness would inevitably suffer. Opting out causes your influence to become almost entirely curtailed, and your ability to accomplish things, which almost always requires interdependent action, to become almost extinguished.

Peter Drucker may have summarised it best when he suggested that 'no leadership education is complete until it is grounded in the political realities of organisational life'.

# Limited access to stakeholders

*One way to exert power and influence in the world of internal organisational politics is to make yourself relatively unavailable to people who see you as an important stakeholder in what they are doing. If someone is limiting your access to them, and you need that access to make progress or to check on decisions or plans you are developing, you will need some political agility to get yourself in front of your stakeholder.*

## First, think:

- How often do other people at your level meet with this stakeholder? How does this compare to your access? Is their access both formal and informal? How does the stakeholder allocate access?

- What is your personality and style like when compared to the stakeholder's? Are there any potential factors which you think might be limiting your access?

- When you are offered access, how do you prepare for the time you do spend with the stakeholder? How do you prioritise the content of those meetings?

- How political is your organisation? Do you feel you are well respected generally within the organisation?

- Is your group suffering through your limited access? What ideas do you have to reduce the impact on your group?

# Ideas for action

## Access is important and you must obtain it

In many organisations there is huge competition for 'face time' and 'mind space' with influential stakeholders. Part of your responsibility to your team is to make sure that you get at a minimum your fair share of this time. This may require you to engage in office politics. Once you have your time it is vital that you use it well and to good effect. This means you must be diligent in your preparation so that you use that meeting to its fullest potential.

## Stakeholders respond to confident managers

Being confident and assertive with senior stakeholders is not easy for newly promoted managers. However, even if you don't feel confident, you should try to project confidence. Influential stakeholders tend to be confident people and tend to respond better to confident assertion than to diffident individuals. Many of us gain confidence and feel better equipped when we have benefited from development through training, coaching or reading books. Do what is necessary to make yourself confident.

## Plan carefully for the time you get

Decide exactly what you want from each meeting and create an agenda for yourself. If you're unsure about what you should be covering, check with your mentor. Make notes to bring into the meeting with you – you don't want to forget to say any of the important things. Share with other influencers questions you have prepared to make sure you are asking the right things.

## Use your mentor

Use your mentor (or anyone with the skill set you need) to help you rehearse for the meeting. It's easy to underestimate the value of rehearsing a difficult conversation. Sometimes just the act of rehearsal gives a confidence boost and helps you prepare for the obstacles you might encounter. Mentors may even be able to help with gaining access to the stakeholder.

## Get in with the gatekeepers

In many organisations senior figures are protected by 'gatekeepers', both formal and informal. The formal gatekeepers may be assistants or junior managers, while the informal ones will be trusted colleagues. It's helpful to build good relationships with the gatekeepers who guard your stakeholder. This may help you to get the access you want when you need it. Also observe carefully what your colleagues do to gain access to senior stakeholders. The informal 'inner circle' may be what you need to penetrate, and members may depend on sharing the interests or hobbies of the trusted advisors who run the circle. In some organisations the key may be golf, in others it may running or mountaineering, while in many others it's as simple as being available for lunch or drinks after work.

## Make an impact, create a network

Think about what you can do to be noticed by the stakeholders to whom you need access. For example, take opportunities to make well-crafted presentations in meetings at which they are present or include them on the circulation list of thoughtful, innovative ideas that have come to you. When you read an interesting article or industry trend you may wish to pass that on to key influencers within your organisation.

Use professional networking opportunities such as LinkedIn sites, special interest groups, industry conferences or online forums to become connected with people whom you might want to influence or who might open doors for you.

Within your own organisation commit time to building a personal network. Seek people out using the excuse of your new position, making sure you have an 'elevator pitch' which is short and impactful and tells them what you want them to know about you.

When you meet people with whom you want to stay connected, invest more time in maintaining a good relationship. For example, allocating an hour out of each week to make phone calls, have coffee or seek out this important network may pay dividends in your future.

### Develop and perfect your influencing skills

When you do gain access to the stakeholder, pay attention to their style and behaviour. If, for example, they seem to prefer detail and logic and seem self-contained, you might in future want to offer material in advance which is set out thoughtfully and accompanied by data-based analysis. If, however, the stakeholder is gregarious, spontaneous and collaborative, that sort of person will probably prefer to respond to you in the moment and is less likely to pre-read before a meeting.

This does not mean you do not prepare for the meeting; what it means is that you prepare your views and ideas but offer them when the moment is right in the meeting. The key to influencing is flexing your style to reflect how the other person likes to be influenced rather than trying to influence everyone in the way you like to be influenced.

An important aspect of influencing is personal credibility. A simple way to build your credibility is to dress and act in the manner of an influential senior executive in the organisation. If you look and act the part, people will assume you can be the part.

### Remember you have a responsibility to the team

In competitive internal environments reduced access to stakeholders can damage your team. Your responsibility as a manager, whatever your personal limitations, is to represent your team well within the organisation.

# Building your personal brand

*In the increasingly competitive world of business, where the pressure to perform and succeed can be huge, having a personal brand – standing for something – is a useful way to differentiate yourself from others. It is not a substitute for performance but it is an excellent additional aspect of the successful manager.*

## First, think:

- What are the key strengths or skills for which you want to be known, and how are you currently perceived within your team and organisation? Are you happy with these perceptions?
- What are the important professional things about you that you want other people to recognise and especially associate with you? Is everything about you aligned to your brand?
- When you think of the image you want to project about yourself, is it currently both credible and sustainable? What is valued in your organisation?
- How is your style or way of working different from those of your team members? How would you like it to be different?
- Do other people in your group positively stand out within your organisation? Why? Who is seen to be successful within your organisation? What attributes do they have?
- Are your ambitions stretching but realistic? To whom do your ambitions represent a threat?

# Ideas for action

## Having a personal brand makes a difference

Within a competitive organisation a strong personal brand is an important way to differentiate yourself from those with whom you are in competition. In every organisation there is room for only a limited number of people to succeed and to move upwards. If your ambition is to be one of these people then a credible, sustainable personal brand will be a significant step forward.

## Successful brands are built on strengths

Successful brands don't try to paper over cracks. They also set you apart from your competitors in some way. There are two aspects to brand appeal: one is rational and tangible and relates to what you do; the other is emotional and intangible and relates to how you behave. The first is important because it relates to your professionalism. However, it is the second that is the differentiator. How people respond to you at an emotional level is what will cause you to stand out from the rest. This is what is called your 'brand essence'.

## People will judge you, at least in part, on what you do

How they judge you and what they judge you on will depend on what's valued in your organisation. It may be a qualification, field experience, past performance, craft skills, business or personal presentation skills and/or performance metrics. If you feel you have any shortfalls here, you should address them. You must be confident that people will see you as being tangibly good at what you do.

## People will differentiate based on your 'brand essence'

Your 'brand essence' is those things about you that make you distinctive and valuable. These are intangible but will include concepts such as your personal presence, charisma, energy, loyalty to the organisation, openness, emotional intelligence and attractiveness as an individual.

These are the parts of your personal brand where you make choices about how you want others to see you. Think carefully about what you want to focus on. Where are you trying to take your career? You can't be all things to all people – this will only dilute your message. So, what sort of person could you credibly be who would succeed in your organisation?

## Be honest and realistic in developing your brand

It might be helpful to start this process by writing down your tangible and intangible strengths. Map these onto what you know the organisation values. Think of successful individuals in the organisation and write down the strengths they bring to the organisation. Where are their strengths different from yours? What can you learn from this?

Once you have decided on your brand personality – which is how others see you – then make sure that everything about you is aligned with this personality. For example, if you would like to project your brand personality as a creative innovator, don't dress like an accountant.

One route to a personal brand is to align yourself carefully with the brand image the organisation wants to project. Here, you are presenting yourself as a defining example of the organisation's identity. Another route is to choose consciously to stand apart from the brand image of the organisation and to stand for something different but important to what the brand does. For example, if you are an HR professional working in an organisation which is predominantly concerned with performance, you may choose to stand out by being the person who champions performance through relationship building and emotional intelligence.

Having decided what you want to stand for, you must consistently offer this image to the organisation. This is why it's so important that your brand image is built on your strengths and is both credible and sustainable.

## Network, get connected

When you have decided what your brand image is going to be you must bring that image to the organisation. Get introduced to people who, in your view, will find your brand image exciting and relevant.

## Be prepared for challenges

In a competitive environment colleagues may respond to attempts you make to differentiate yourself. They may undermine the brand you are trying to create; they may try to cast doubts on your credibility. Your brand image has to be robust enough to withstand this sort of attack. If, at the first sign of competition, you are seen not to be what you say you are, your brand image will be immediately damaged.

Your personal brand can be a vital part of how you are perceived. Like brands in a supermarket, your brand image will take time to establish. Once established it can only change incrementally and over time. Sudden changes in brand images are rarely well received.

# Getting a decision

*For many of us, life at work moves at a very fast pace. Therefore, getting decisions is vital because without decisions that pace can't be maintained. So what happens if you can't get a decision made when you desperately need it?*

## First, think:

- Where is the barrier? How does the person you are trying to influence like to make decisions? Have you given them everything they need to make the decision the way they like to?
- What is your relationship with the key decision maker? Are you well connected to others who might be able to influence the decision maker? What about your boss – is there a route through your boss and around the barrier?
- Is your request within 'normal' boundaries or is it an extraordinary request? Are you asking for a decision more quickly than normal?
- What are the ramifications for you and/or the business if the decision isn't made or if you don't get the decision you would like?
- Do you generally find difficulty in getting decisions made? Is the organisation typically slow at decision making?
- Do you suspect organisational politics at play? Might this delay be at least partly caused by someone pursuing personal goals?

## Ideas for action

### Decision making is at the heart of every organisation

But each case will be different; some organisations are adept at making decisions while others are more ponderous. The same is true for individuals within organisations. You need first to identify exactly who or what represents the barrier, then decide whether the barrier is benign or malign. If it's simply a matter of adapting your style to suit the individual from whom you are trying to extract a decision, or if the decision you need is stuck within internal processes, then the barrier you need to remove is broadly benign. However, if there is political manoeuvring or if personal agendas are at work, the barrier may be more malign and more difficult to remove. What you do next depends on what you discover.

## Remove benign barriers to decisions

So let's take the easier one first. Think about your preferences and those of the individual(s) you are trying to influence. You need to be sure you are communicating the background to and the need for a decision in a style they would want. Is the decision maker generally open, outgoing and energetic? If so, then your communication style needs to match their approach to business. They will more likely respond to a quick synopsis and high-energy brainstorming-type activities together with you. Don't give people like this reams of paper with data to analyse, because, if you do, you are creating the barrier to their decision making.

If the decision maker is analytical, data orientated and thoughtful, you will need to have carefully thought through the content of the materials you provide. If the information is absent or inadequate, again you have created the barrier to decision making.

Some decision makers are people orientated and will need to understand the impact of their decision on the people whom it will affect. If you don't demonstrate to the decision maker that you have considered the human dimension, then you should not be surprised if a decision is slow in coming.

## Deal with decision-averse people differently

Once you are reassured that you are providing the decision maker with the right material in the right way but you are still not getting a decision, then something else to consider is whether the decision maker is generally decision averse.

Examine their history of decision making: is it slow or inconsistent? With decision-averse people you will need to remind them regularly of the urgency attached to the decision. You may also need to recruit others to help the decision maker see and accept the need to make the decision.

However people like to make decisions, few people like to be rushed. Make sure that, regardless of how the individual likes you to communicate with them, at a minimum you give them an appropriate length of time within which to make the decision. Are you seen as someone who demands decisions with short lead times? If this is your reputation, you may inadvertently have alienated people to the point where they are consciously (or unconsciously) delaying decisions you need made.

One thing about which you must be absolutely clear is the timeframe within which the decision must be made. If this window is missed, the consequences to the team and the organisation must be made plain.

## Understand where power and influence lie

Examine the power and influence the decision maker has. Sometimes people who lack power slow down their decision-making process because they lack confidence and do not have the influence to defend the decision robustly. An individual like this may need you to persuade key stakeholders of the rightness of the decision before they commit themselves to making it.

## Boss barriers are harder to remove

If the barrier is your boss then the challenge is more immediate and often more complex. Decision making will be part of the wider relationship you have, so be sure you understand that relationship's nuances. A boss is more likely to give you a quick decision if you are seen as credible and trustworthy. If you are seen as overtly personally ambitious or careless then the decisions you request will be subject to much closer scrutiny.

## Consider the politics

Organisational politics will often influence decision making. In an organisation where politics are an important part of daily life, people need to look at decisions from a number of different perspectives. For example, do they think you have a hidden or open agenda (personal or organisational)? If such an agenda is felt to exist then don't be surprised if the decision maker wants to pause and consider all the implications before making the decision. Sometimes your reputation alone is enough for the decision maker to expect a political agenda and therefore to take longer in making the decision.

Decision makers who are themselves actively engaged in organisational politics will always want to make sure that they understand any political consequences of the decision. This will take time. If this decision is particularly important to you, then you need to invest the time in advance to think through the political consequences and share them with the decision maker. If this is done well it will help reassure the decision maker and clear the path to a decision.

## Examine and understand the bigger picture

Finally, don't forget that the decision you seek may be part of a wider picture. You may not be aware of bigger issues being considered which may impact on your decision in an unexpected way.

# Organisational politics

*Every organisation has politics; politics exist where there are two or more people working interdependently together. The choice isn't whether you get involved or not. The choice is how you get involved. You can, however, decide to retain your integrity and play office politics wisely.*

## First, think:

- How acceptable are individuals' personal ambitions, hidden agendas and covert activities within your organisation?
- What about you – do you think of politics as a dirty word? Or do you see the potential for politics to be a force for good? Do you relish playing politics or prefer just to observe?
- What are your ambitions? How important are organisational politics to your achieving these ambitions?
- Are you positively inclined towards the organisation? What's your history with your organisation and with organisational politics in general? Have you had your fingers burnt – has this made you cautious or damaged your confidence?
- Do you have a lot of power within your organisation? What type(s) of power do you have? Are you good at influencing?
- Where does your personal balance lie between being self-orientated and orientated towards the organisation's objectives?

# Ideas for action

## It's almost impossible not to be involved in organisational politics

Politics exist whenever interdependent action is needed. There are always hidden and open personal and organisational agendas – so there are always politics. The majority of people automatically associate 'organisational politics' with negative behaviour. However, organisational politics themselves are neither good nor bad; it's how people play that is beneficial or harmful. So, once you accept that organisational politics are always around, you can make the decision to engage with politics in a way which is positive and constructive. You can be political and act with integrity.

Once you've thought about your own responses to organisational politics, you then need to think about why you have those responses: has anything happened to you in the past to colour your view? Is your organisation's approach to politics particularly manipulative? Your answers to these two fundamental questions will help you to understand and, if necessary, change your relationship with office politics. It's important that you have a constructive view of organisational politics, otherwise it's possible that your behaviour will encourage others in your team to engage in self-interested political activity while also potentially holding back your career progress.

When you observe office politics you will quickly see there are different types of players. There are those who act with integrity and who use office politics to help meet the organisation's objectives; there are others who are Machiavellian and use office politics to help achieve their own personal ambitions; still others are naïve victims of office politics; a few try simply to hide away and ignore the politics going on around them – these are the organisational hermits. Your role as a manager is to make sure you understand which of these roles you are currently playing (and how to get from there to a point where you can play office politics with integrity) and to help the people in your team move to that same point. You also have a role in appreciating and taking into account where key stakeholders are on this political map. Understanding this will help you to defend against the negative political activity of others.

## Some people are more drawn to office politics than others

Even those drawn to politics will become more cautious if they have had their fingers burnt. Reflecting on what has happened in your political past, both to yourself and to others around you, will help you to understand the approach you have had to organisational politics and whether that approach needs to change.

Critical to how individuals approach and play office politics is how they feel about the organisation itself. If you feel good about your organisation and feel it has treated you fairly, your political activity is likely to be positive. On the other hand, if you feel bad about your organisation, how it treats you and others, then your political activity may be negative. As a manager this is important. By assessing an individual's relationship with the organisation, you can anticipate what their approach to office politics is going to be. You can also change their approach to office politics by helping them to review and change how they feel about the organisation.

## Your primary instruments are use of power and ability to influence

There are several sources of power: information power, positional power, coercive power, charismatic power, reward power, gatekeeper power and particularly the power provided by the management of resources. Knowing which of these powers are available to you and others and who holds how much of each power source will be an important first step in your political activity.

Influence is rather different. Anybody can influence anybody else if their influencing skills are well enough developed. The thing about influencing is that it changes people's attitudes which means that, in the long term, it provides more sustainable results than the use of power. As with power, there are a number of different approaches to influencing. It's important to choose the approach which is most appropriate to each situation. This can be difficult because each of us tends to have a preferred influencing style which we use regardless of the situation.

Typical influencing styles include, at one end of the spectrum, providing facts, persuasive reasoning, rationalising, asserting and negotiating, and at the other end collaborating, bridging, inspiring and visioning. Be aware at which end of this spectrum you prefer to operate and try to develop your influencing skills elsewhere on the spectrum. Matching your influencing style not only to the situation but also to the individual and the organisation's culture is likely to get you more success.

## Self-orientation breeds divisiveness

The most divisive aspect of politics happens when an individual's approach is predominantly self-orientated. A short-term gain that is achieved via self-orientated methods may work (and indeed, may be appropriate) sometimes; however, your long-term career aspirations are far more likely to be met by using politics to help achieve organisational goals.

# Managing up or across

*Influencing without authority is one of the most subtle skills to master. However, because all of us at some point want or need to manage up or across our organisation, all of us need to understand how to influence without authority. Properly done, it helps you to get what you want while maintaining integrity.*

## First, think:

- What is your professional relationship with the person you need to influence? From your knowledge, how does this person like to be influenced? Do they respond well to facts and logic or do they prefer intuitive arguments and passion? Do they want a lot of detail or do they prefer being presented with the summary?
- What, exactly, do you want from the encounter? What attitude, decision or action do you want to influence?
- Do you believe this person is open to being influenced? Are you the best choice of influencer for this person and for this course of action or decision? How much access do you have?
- Where is the person's self-interest in this? What are the likely objections this person might present? How can you present what you want to happen as something that will help the person to meet their or their team's goal or objective?
- Are others likely to be trying to influence the person about the same issue or opportunity? Who are these other influencers? What are your influencing strengths and weaknesses compared to those of your competition?
- What happens if you fail to influence as you intend?

# Ideas for action

### Influence people their way – not yours

The way to influence somebody is to do it in the way *they* would like to be influenced rather than in the way *you* might like to be. Just as we are drawn to people who are similar to us, we also communicate with people as we would like to be communicated with. The first important step in the influencing process is to think about how the person would like to be influenced.

### Learn to influence one-to-many

Often situations aren't just about one person's decision; you may need to influence several different stakeholders. If you are influencing a number of people, you need to think through the preferences for each person you want to influence. For example, does the individual prefer detached logic? Is he or she very protective of the team? Is the individual competitive? Does he or she want a lot of detail or the big picture? Once you have built up a picture of their preferences, you can start to plan how to approach the person.

### Treat people you know and people you do not know differently

Sometimes knowing well the person you are trying to influence will be an advantage: after all, you are familiar with their likes and dislikes. However, it is also true that any relationship has some emotional baggage attached to it and sometimes this baggage can get in the way of your attempts to influence. Equally, trying to influence someone you don't know at all is difficult, but at least there is no history to interfere with your attempt.

### Your success is linked to the amount of preparation you have done

Rushing into an attempt to influence somebody can backfire. In many situations you have just one shot at influencing someone, so it's important to get it right the first time. Your first attempt to influence will colour the impression the other person has of you and the situation, making later attempts to influence more difficult.

Think through the likely arguments you will face or the barriers you may encounter. It is important to plan your responses: reacting spontaneously to an argument risks heated or inappropriate reactions. You will respond better to arguments that you encounter if you have a clear idea both of your ideal outcome and of a 'good enough' outcome. Think, too, about whether you are trying to influence one single decision or if you have a longer-term target in mind where this encounter is the first step in a journey.

Consider who else might be trying to influence the same person on the same issue but in a different direction. You will need to think about how you would challenge or respond to the argument they may put forward. If any of these people are better influencers or better placed to influence than you, then you need to have a strategy in place which will maximise the strengths you do have. Your strengths may be the arguments you can put forward, the relationship you have with that individual or even the relationships you have with people close to that individual.

## Time your attempts thoughtfully

If you want to give yourself the best chance of influencing successfully, then give some thought to when and where you will make your attempt. It needs to be somewhere where both of you can feel comfortable and at a time when both of you are able to discuss the situation without time pressure. Allow the person to be in their own space if that is what they would prefer. Be aware of their body language and non-verbal cues (both before and during the conversation). If you sense any resistance being brought into the meeting, be prepared to postpone your attempt until a better opportunity presents itself.

Often, you are attempting to influence not an individual but a group – for example, in a meeting. The old adage that most decisions don't get made in the meeting but get made before the meeting is true. So you should always attempt to do your influencing individually and in advance. However, there will be times when you will need to influence or persuade a group. This is more about your powers of persuasion than it is about their individual preferences. This is about presenting your argument in your way to the very best of your ability – with confidence and impact.

## Have fallbacks and options

Finally, think in advance about what happens if decisions don't go your way. How important is this decision to you personally and to your career? It's sometimes reassuring to know in advance that even if you fail in your attempt to influence, it isn't going to be the end of the world. Remember you can lose the battle yet still win the war.

# Being micro-managed

*While you are learning how to do a job it may be appropriate for your manager to pay close attention to what you do and how you do it. But as you grow in confidence and ability this same previously supportive behaviour can feel stifling. Few people flourish while being unnecessarily micro-managed. How do you persuade your manager to behave differently without alienating them?*

## First, think:

- Do you think that your boss believes that micro-managing you is in your interest or in their own interest? When you honestly appraise your own approach and performance, are you willing and able to do the job without requiring micro-managing? Can you offer any evidence for this?
- Is your boss's approach to managing you different from the way in which others are managed? If so, why is it different? What opinion do you believe your boss has of you and what would you want that opinion to be?
- Is your boss under threat in any way? How is your boss's performance measured? Is your boss micro-managed?
- Have others noticed or commented on the way you are managed?
- How is the way you are managed affecting you? Do you have in your mind a better model for managing you and do you have any evidence that this model has worked well, either in this organisation or elsewhere?
- What is the best way to raise your concerns with your boss? Does your boss welcome feedback from team members?

# Ideas for action

## You have to understand context

Important to address in this dilemma is understanding context: does this person manage you in a significantly different way from the way in which others are managed? This will help tell you whether this is the manager's general style or whether this approach is specifically directed at you. Some managers have a reputation for micro-managing. You may want to check with your colleagues whether they are feeling as you do. If your manager micro-manages everybody, it's worth talking to other people managed by him or her to try to develop a group approach to the problem.

Mismanagement of this sort can rapidly undermine the morale of the team and affect the team's performance. If the manager is relatively new but has at least got his or her feet under the table and is still micro-managing the group, an honest and open conversation has to take place. Carefully plan with your fellow team members what the feedback will be and what your proposed ideas for resolution are. It will be important to think about who will lead this communication and when, where and how the meeting will take place.

There are times when a manager, especially one under pressure from above, may micro-manage not because the individual or team needs it but because the manager feels vulnerable. This may be a short-term and understandable thing and, as a team, you may wish to support your manager through this period by allowing this approach, even though it is inappropriate.

## There are times when micro-management is an appropriate approach

For example, when individuals are new to a role or trying to acquire new skills for a project, a manager may feel the need to stay very close to a team member and the team member may appreciate the attention. An experienced manager may initially choose to manage someone new to a role very closely; however, this is short term and the manager will withdraw as soon as the individual shows themselves to be capable. A less experienced manager may overstay their welcome. This is often because they lack confidence in themselves rather than in the individual.

## Informed, objective advice is always valuable

Seek the opinions of your mentor or of a trusted colleague, ideally one who has managed you in the past. Once you have described how you are being managed, ask them whether they think it is appropriate. You may get feedback concerning your preferences about how you like to be managed. It may be that you like freedom and empowerment and you see micro-management where others simply see appropriate supervision. If, together, you decide that you could be managed better, the conversation with your mentor or colleague can turn to how best to influence your line manager. It helps if you can be clear about how you would prefer to be managed and how you think your performance would improve if you were managed differently.

## Consider why YOU are micro-managed

If it's clear that you really are managed more closely than anyone else then you need to think about why this might be. It's either about the relationship or about your competence. A relationship in which your line manager feels the need to micro-manage you sounds like one in which trust either has never been present or has disappeared. Have you done anything to cause this person's trust in you to nosedive? Think about your reliability, your consistency, your communication with and your loyalty to your manager as starting points for your reflection. If you decide that trust is the issue, you will need a strategy to rebuild the manager's trust in you. If the issue is about competence, you need to address the gaps and show you can perform to the required standards. Both of these courses of action will need you to speak with your manager to present a plan which addresses your shortfalls.

Using a directive style in an appropriate situation can feel supportive and encouraging to the person being managed; overuse of this same style when it is no longer appropriate can quickly feel stifling and inhibiting. If you feel stifled you owe it to yourself to explore why and to take action.

# Someone who is holding you back

*It is frustrating to know that you are able, that you are seen as cred-ible, and yet to be held back by someone. Whatever the reason for this, you will want to be able to realise your ambitions and take con-trol over your future. To do so you will need to understand not just who is holding you back but why they are doing it.*

## First, think:

- What reasons for holding you back might the individual have?
- Who has to collude with this person in holding you back – either by actively helping or by passively standing by – and why might they do so?
- Have you done anything to cause this person not to trust you?
- If you achieve your goals, who stands to gain or to lose among your colleagues?
- Are you seen by others as predominantly self-interested? Overtly ambitious?
- Are there others whose views might shine a light on the situation? How can you approach some or all of these people without exacerbating the problem?
- What happens if you do nothing? What are the downside risks to taking action? What power or influence does the individual have?
- Can you readily move out of the individual's orbit? Are there others who would value you more and would welcome you joining their team?

# Ideas for action

## Examine closely the situation at hand

Organisational life is complex and hectic; situations can sometimes appear to be personal and purposeful when in fact there are innocent explanations. You have to be sure that you have considered all possibilities before reaching the degree of certainty that allows you to act. Think especially about where that individual's self-interest might lie. If there is no self-interest, why would someone want to hold you back? Be clear about what exactly you are being held back from.

## You must first be clear about the intent and why the intent exists

Then, your first decision will be whether you intend to do anything about it. This will depend upon the severity of the impact on you, the power and influence of the person you feel is holding you back, your own power and influence, and your willingness and ability to do what is necessary to respond to this threat. Be honest with yourself about how professionally competent you are: could the individual holding you back be doing so for your own protection? Are you reaching too far and too fast for your ability? If your reputation within the organisation is one of overt ambition or self-interest, do be sure that you are indeed being inappropriately held back. Having evaluated the circumstances, you may decide to do nothing. If this is the choice you make, be sure to think through the likely consequences for you and your career.

## Develop a plan of action

You now need to think about your history with this person. Why are they trying to hold you back and what do they have to gain? People sometimes consciously or unconsciously hold others back because they perceive them to be a threat to their own careers. If you believe the individual is acting unconsciously, your action may be to bring their behaviour to their attention and ask them to consider the implications of what they are doing. Or you may choose to enlist the help of someone else who has a good relationship with the person and is able to challenge their behaviour.

If, however, you believe this person is acting consciously to hold you back, prepare well: think about what you would like to say, anticipate their responses and reactions and be prepared for the exchange to become confrontational. Remember that even if you decide the individual is acting consciously, you may still choose to enlist the help of someone else who is better placed to challenge and address the behaviour.

## Is your own behaviour contributing to a competitive relationship with this person?

You have to accept responsibility for the effects of your attitude or approach on any relationship. In short, you may be part of the problem.

It may be that the professional environment in which you operate is too political or politically malicious. If the actions that are upsetting you are considered to be normal in your organisation, it may be inappropriate of you to expect anything else or to expect a resolution.

It can be upsetting to feel you are being held back and people who are upset can make poor decisions. Seek feedback from key stakeholders as to your competence and credibility within the organisation. If you have a wide network and are well regarded within that network, then in the long run the views of the majority about your ability will overcome the view of the person trying to hold you back. This approach, though long term, avoids risks associated with addressing the issue. You need to make sure your efforts and results are visible to a wide audience.

If you try and fail to address this or if you decide it cannot be readily addressed, the option remains for you to seek an internal move or even an external one. Happiness is a key element of success in the workplace.

# 7

**Challenges for yourself**

All managers, at some points in their careers, receive difficult feedback: you hear a message you don't want to hear about yourself, or others confirm something about you that you haven't wanted to examine or explore too closely. Successful managers are able to receive difficult personal feedback, synthesise it and use it to make themselves stronger and better.

Some of the biggest dilemmas that managers encounter are not actually with other people or with demands made on their skills or competence. Often managers can deal well with these tangible challenges. For many managers, the biggest challenges are those far more intangible challenges around self-awareness. How do you best respond to the highly personal: challenges that seem to be aimed directly at you, not as a professional but as an individual?

Self-awareness helps you to cope with challenges that seem to be aimed at you personally, because it gives you a clear idea of who you are and what you are about. When you are self-aware you know what is important to you; you know how you like to work and how you like to interact with others; you know your strengths as an individual and you know where you have areas for improvement. When you are self-aware like this, feedback from others can be valuable because it is feedback offered to someone who is self-informed.

If you lack self-awareness then you have far fewer ways in which to evaluate the feedback given to you: is it right or not? Is it useful or not? Is it accurate or not? Your temptation may be to embrace the positive feedback and ignore the negative. It is unlikely that this will be in your long-term best interests.

# Receiving difficult feedback

*Critical to a successful career is the willingness to receive construc-*
*tive feedback well, even if what you hear is uncomfortable. Feedback*
*is an important mechanism through which you can grow, learn and*
*develop. Receiving feedback well will demonstrate your maturity and*
*will encourage open dialogue by modelling best behaviour.*

## First, think:

- Are you aware of how you tend to react to constructive critical feedback? Are you defensive or open minded?
- Is giving and receiving challenging feedback a norm within your team? What about within your organisation's culture?
- Do you agree with the feedback being given to you? Who is the feedback provider? Do you respect him or her? Is the feedback given in a way that reflects an understanding of you and how you like to work?
- How difficult are you to give feedback to? What can you do to make things easier for the feedback provider?
- Who are the people whose feedback you would trust and respect? Do you actively seek feedback from them?
- Is this particular critical feedback challenging your career or in any other way serious or limiting? What is the motivation of the feedback provider?
- What is your reputation within your organisation? Are you seen as credible and successful?

# Ideas for action

## Remember that feedback is a highly individual thing

Some people love it and want it by the bucketload, while others prefer feedback in very small doses and only from people they know very well and for whom they have lots of respect. Also, in some organisations feedback is a prevalent part of the culture, while in others it is given once a year (if that) during performance reviews. Remember, too, that people and organisations differ in formality; some are more formal and conservative while others are much less structured and more open. Some people and organisations are more circumspect, some are more direct. Feedback must be appropriate both to the recipient and to the culture.

## Be open to feedback

Bearing all of that in mind before receiving feedback may improve your openness to the feedback. The responsibility of the feedback provider is to offer the difficult feedback in a way in which they believe is likely to make it most acceptable to you. It's more difficult to see value in feedback that is inappropriately provided, but you still have a responsibility to listen actively and reflect properly on what you have heard. Remember that receiving difficult feedback well is different from agreeing with it. You must be able to receive difficult feedback graciously even if, having considered it carefully, you later decide that you do not agree with all of it.

## The style for giving feedback should change according to the organisation's culture, the situation and the individual recipient

The person giving feedback may choose to be informal and impromptu when providing feedback that is less critical in nature; they may find a more formal environment better suited to feedback which is particularly critical. It may be far better to set up a specific time and private space in which to give feedback that might be badly received or that is highly personal.

## Feedback is most powerful when it's timely

Giving you feedback weeks after the event will not serve you or the feedback provider very well; the impact and the relevance are long gone. This is often difficult for managers with very busy diaries who must ensure they make time for regular feedback with their reports. However, if done well, it's a powerful tool to contribute to high performance and a positive culture.

## Make sure you are clear about the ramifications of this feedback

What is this difficult feedback about? If your credibility is already established within your organisation and this feedback is simply pointing out ways to improve even further, it may help to reflect at leisure on what is being suggested. If, however, the feedback is pointing out something fundamental with long-term relevance, then however much you might want to resist what you are hearing, you really must consider immediately and very carefully what your next steps will be. Again, it may help to gauge the opinion of a trusted mentor or close colleague. If the long-term ramifications of this feedback represent a significant barrier to your career or progression within the organisation, you should take this feedback as a helpful stimulus to serious reflection on what you do and how you do it.

## Ask the feedback giver to provide structure

Particularly when receiving difficult feedback, it helps the giver and the receiver if there is some structure to the feedback provided. Sometimes asking questions is a good way of opening the door to a good exchange of views. Asking questions is especially useful when the individual is withdrawn or defensive and finds interpersonal communication challenging. It's also a great way to get clarity or detail when you receive challenging feedback. Particularly if you find yourself becoming defensive, asking some genuinely open questions may also give some breathing space to help your defensive wall come down as well as providing you with important information and context.

Feedback is as much about the giver as it is about the receiver. If you sense that the provider has a personal agenda, you might be suspicious of their motives; however, it doesn't automatically mean the feedback is inaccurate. If you receive feedback which makes you uneasy, it's always worth validating it by discussing it with someone who knows you and the situation well and who has your respect. Hearing the feedback confirmed by such a person may well cause you to treat it more seriously.

# Situations where you don't know the answer

*Every day managers find themselves in situations where they don't know the answer. Modern business life tends to create complex challenges where answers are not a simple yes or no. So sometimes not knowing is entirely appropriate. The important thing is not to allow this to affect your confidence in yourself. There are times when answering without full certainty is entirely appropriate. The trick is to know what you are expected to know.*

## First, think:

- What are the expectations of your questioners? Are their expectations reasonable?
- What is your standing with the questioner and with any listeners? Might there be an impact on your standing or reputation if you answer incompletely or inaccurately? Do you have to answer now?
- Think carefully about your own position: if you can't answer fully, why not? In your view, is it understandable and appropriate that you can't answer fully?
- If you can answer fully but choose not to, then why are you electing to withhold information? What are the consequences if or when it is discovered that you have withheld information? Should you admit to knowledge that you can't share?
- Think about the question or request for information itself: is it appropriate? Might the questioner have a political or self-serving agenda in asking the question? Is the question valid but might the reasons for asking it be invalid?

# Ideas for action

## Nobody can be expected to know the answer to everything

The first thing to explore is whether you should be expected to know the answer to this question. Many people see confidence all around them yet feel little themselves. What they do not realise is the extent to which someone else's apparent confidence may be bravado. People often resemble ducks: calm on the surface but paddling like mad underneath.

## Understand the implications of not knowing

Nevertheless, we should acknowledge that not knowing the answers to questions can cause great distress to individuals who have a low sense of self-esteem or self-worth. A lack of self-esteem regularly leads to crippling self-doubt. For these people confidence is a fragile thing, easily undermined. If you are one of these people, there are steps you can take to develop your sense of self-worth and your assertiveness. Examples might be to change your negative self-talk to positive, having a personal coach at work, counselling outside work, and even reading from the vast amount of literature written on this subject.

## Be clear about context

If you are new in your role or new to the organisation, it is understandable that there will be areas where you can't answer as well as a more experienced manager might. In this situation you need to find ways to bring yourself up to speed as quickly as possible: commit time to finding out about the organisation, about the role and about the expectations people have of you. It might even be that a structured management development intervention – perhaps even a qualification of some sort – will give you the knowledge-based confidence you want.

Even experienced managers will have parts of their role where they are less knowledgeable. It's always risky to bluff; often an admission that you don't know something, followed by a swift commitment to finding out, is actually more impressive than trying to bluff or bluster your way past a question. Especially if you already have a good track record within the organisation, being fallible from time to time is likely to make you more rather than less credible with your colleagues.

Sometimes you won't know the answer because the answer is a composite of knowledge and understanding from across the team. If this is the case, the best way to get to that knowledge and understanding is for you to open the question up to the wider group. You need to understand what is most likely to help you and the team meet the goals and objectives – to answer as fully as you can, admitting that you do not have a complete answer or solution; or not to answer at all, because you don't have a complete answer.

## You can't always tell what you know

There will be times when you can answer a question but you feel it is inappropriate to share the information with the questioner. This may be for reasons of business confidentiality or perhaps because you are protecting someone who has confided in you. If you are sure it is appropriate not to answer, then you should explain that you can answer but choose not to, and give your reasons. There will be other times when you are asked questions which are simply too big or uncertain for you to be able to answer. Even though people expect managers to know a great deal, it's OK to say 'I don't know' or 'I don't have a view on that yet'. For example, managers are often asked to predict the future; the wise manager knows not to try. The critical skill for managers is to know whether or not it's appropriate to know the answer to the question being asked.

# Dealing with your own mistakes and poor decisions

*Managers have a wide arc of people they influence and who influence them. Therefore, when mistakes happen they often involve several people and affect many people. No one is perfect. So how do you deal with the fallout of a poor decision or a mistake you have made?*

## First, think:

- Exactly how big is the error you have made? Is it business critical? How many people does it affect? Is it recoverable?
- Are the ramifications of the poor decision in the public domain?
- How many people were involved in contributing to the decision?
- Why was the poor decision made? Was the process flawed or was it simply the wrong decision?
- What can you learn from the process to help you in the future? Have you made other, similar poor decisions like this before? Is there a pattern to when and how your judgement fails you?
- How do you feel about your part in the decision-making process? Has this affected your self-confidence?
- What are the implications for you personally once the mistake is public and your role understood?
- Have you examined the benefits and drawbacks of revealing your mistake? To what audience would you reveal your mistake?

# Ideas for action

## Everybody makes mistakes

An important point to acknowledge is that we are all human and we all make mistakes. The successful manager learns from mistakes (and therefore doesn't repeat the same mistake) and is able to be forgiving of themselves and others for mistakes that are made.

## Decide how bad the error might be

If we take as a given that we all make mistakes, then you should reflect on this: what is the scale of this mistake and what is your pattern of making poor decisions in the past? You need to examine whether the ramifications of this mistake are far reaching or have a big impact on the business. Also, you need to understand the reasons behind the mistake: is it a typical mistake of yours or is there something new to be learned from this error?

## Decide what you must do once the error is recognised

Once you've thought about the implications of your poor decisions it is important to act. The bigger the mistake the quicker you need to own up. Most mistakes will be revealed in time and, if it becomes clear that you were in error and said nothing, you will do far more damage to yourself (and potentially to the organisation) than you would do if you brought the error to the attention of your manager. If this mistake is typical of the types of mistakes you tend to make then, beyond admitting it, you must take some action to make sure you stop making these types of errors. You must be prepared to meet more anger and resentment if you regularly make the same sorts of mistakes, small or large. Mistakes that have a personal impact on individuals will be harder for them to accept than those that do not affect them individually.

## Don't rush to take or accept all the blame

Many mistakes and poor decisions are joint ventures. In a complex professional world we seldom make unilateral decisions: colleagues, clients and direct reports will all contribute to the decision or the thinking behind the decision. As a manager you are accountable for the mistakes of your people even if you haven't personally made or ratified the poor decision.

When you admit your error to the organisation it's important that you bring with you ways to address or rectify that error and an analysis of the impact of the error. Be able to communicate clearly what happened and why it happened and what can be done to put things right. Even in the face of angry criticism, try not to get defensive but equally don't be a martyr.

## Know what has to change to eradicate this error in the future

When you are reviewing the error or decision it's important that you differentiate between the process that led you there and the choice that you then made. You have to understand whether the process was flawed, which in turn led to the bad choice, or whether the process was good yet, despite this, the choice was wrong. Until you have examined your actions in this way you won't know what you have to address and change.

More common than the huge errors that compromise the business is the mistake or poor decision which has short-term or limited repercussions. Often, these errors, which must be addressed, will not need to be referred up the organisation. What's needed is swift remedial action which persuades your team and others around you that you are able to see, recognise and deal with the mistakes that each of us inevitably makes.

## Restore trust

Part of the fallout from errors of judgement is that the trust that others have in you is damaged. You need to decide in the light of each individual error how best to minimise the effect of that error on the trust of others in you. Mistakes cause people to think you lack competence or perhaps reliability, while hiding mistakes that you have made can look to others like obvious self-interest. All of these impressions will have a negative impact on other people's level of trust in you. The point here is that fallout from errors of judgement can go beyond the impact on the business. Trust is hard-earned and readily lost.

An emotionally intelligent manager is able to see and deal with personal mistakes without letting them destroy their self-confidence or self-esteem or the trust of others. Every manager must walk a fine line between arrogance and being too humble; the other balance to be struck is between being candid about your mistakes and attempting to hide them from the gaze of others. If you can address and correct your mistake, there is usually little need to admit your error to others. There is always a need, though, to learn from your mistakes.

# Feeling under-equipped

*Every one of us feels better equipped for certain parts of our jobs than for others. The view we all need to form is whether there is a dangerous shortfall or an allowable weakness. Key factors in deciding whether you are genuinely under-equipped for your role include examining which of your gaps are business critical, which are a function of inexperience and which can be filled by the skills and competencies of others.*

## First, think:

- What are the gaps you feel you have? Are they critical to your role? Do you feel poorly equipped because of your lack of experience?
- Does your job make different demands on you now than it did in the past? Are you required to perform better in areas where in the past you had little involvement?
- How has this been brought to your attention? Have you received feedback? Do you agree with it?
- What else has changed around you? Have you had a new boss? A new team member? New responsibilities? Have you experienced significant personal or organisational change?
- Is low self-esteem colouring your judgement of your own ability? How objective are you about your strengths and weaknesses?
- Are there aspects of your role for which you are particularly well equipped? Does this highlight your weaknesses in other areas?

# Ideas for action

## Don't set the bar unrealistically high

At times each of us feels that sense of vulnerability associated with feeling under-equipped for what we are setting out to do. In truth it simply isn't credible that any one person can be fully equipped to deal with every aspect of a complex management position. Many people have that feeling of 'imposter syndrome' where they feel inadequate and bound to be found out or discovered. Some managers suffer this in silence while others are more able to admit it to colleagues and in return get support and camaraderie.

There is a balance to be struck here between critical self-analysis (which is a good thing) and an inappropriate sense of inadequacy (which is likely to hinder your performance). Every role has business-critical aspects and 'nice to have' elements. If, upon examination, you discover that some of the centrally important aspects to your role require attention, you have learned something valuable upon which you must act. If, on the other hand, the elements you lack are 'nice to have', you should remember that part of a manager's skill is to use the resources available to make sure that everything is done to the highest possible standards. To do this you may choose to up-skill yourself or access the skills of others in your team. You may find that joining a professional network or taking up an appropriate development opportunity will allow you to address aspects of your job which you feel you need to improve.

## Know how to process feedback

Sometimes a feeling of being under-equipped can stem from feedback received from others. Despite the best efforts of the feedback provider, it is occasionally the case that feedback leads to a feeling of being under-equipped either because of low self-confidence or because of a perceived skills shortfall. If the provider is someone you respect and you take the feedback seriously, you will want to address what you've heard.

## Realistically establish what you should be able to know and do

Your relationship to your role is a critical aspect of feeling under-equipped. If you are new to your role, and particularly if you are new to the organisation, you may feel under-equipped simply because things are done differently or there are different expectations of you. Most people find the first six months of being in a new role or a new organisation to be a steep learning curve; during this time you are bound to feel less confident, which may manifest itself in a feeling of being under-equipped.

There is also a subtle difference between being inexperienced and being under-equipped. In many roles there is really no substitute for 'miles on the clock'. Some people also find it difficult to argue assertively a point to someone who is older or more experienced than them. In both of these cases it's inexperience which is at the root of your discomfort rather than a lack of ability or competence. Your best friend here is self-confidence. Using a coach or mentor to bounce ideas off and get advice from can be very helpful. You will undoubtedly come across people who excel at something where you'd like to improve. Watching 'experts' at work can be enlightening and can spark ideas for your own approach. In time, your own personal experiences will accumulate and you will have the confidence of having 'been there and done that'.

## Acknowledge the impact of change on yourself

The pace of political, social, economic and technological change is such that jobs can change unrecognisably in a short period of time. Again, the trick here is to distinguish between being under-equipped and being caught in a tide of change. The latter requires you to be flexible and prepared to adapt to and adopt new skills and techniques. Big change makes most of us feel uncertain, unprepared and under-equipped. The best managers overcome these feelings and take the steps necessary to be better equipped to work with and through the change.

Notice, too, what else has changed around you. Life changes such as births, marriages, deaths and divorces can all make a difference to how well equipped you feel to do your job at work.

You may, for whatever reason, feel emotionally vulnerable or simply exhausted. Whatever your emotional state, the end result may be a sense of feeling overwhelmed and therefore unable to perform to the standard you would like.

Having a new team member, a new boss or an obstructive colleague or client can all disturb the balance and leave you feeling exposed. A drop in the level of support or positive feedback you receive from bosses or colleagues can also create a sense of unease. Changing dynamics at work can create a sense of imbalance which in turn can leave you feeling under-equipped to meet the demands of your role. An unfortunate fact about the world of business becoming more and more demanding is that such changing dynamics are more frequent now than they might have been in a more stable business environment.

Once you realise you feel under-equipped, an important first step is to isolate why you feel this way: to do this you will need to notice what has changed around you. Understanding that most people feel under-equipped at some time, you need to have objectivity to ensure you are clear about the strengths that you do bring to the party. Self-esteem is built up by sending positive messages to ourselves. It's better to deal with a sense of being under-equipped than it is to live with it. Significant steps towards this are to bridge competency gaps and focus on building up self-esteem.

# The loneliness of management

*As managers climb up the career ladder there is sometimes an increasing feeling of isolation. Management involves having authority over other people. This naturally changes the relationship the manager has with those people. The bigger the management role, the greater the authority and the more influence that power will have on those relationships.*

## First, think:

- Do you need close relationships at work? If so, must they come from the people whom you manage or can this need be met by other colleagues?
- Is your sense of loneliness recent? Does it coincide with a change in your role or responsibilities at work?
- What is it that you miss? Bouncing ideas off people? Having noise around you? Feeling included and involved? Being informed? Who or what met this need in the past?
- Do you feel well connected to your team at work? Is there a sense of camaraderie and belonging within the team? Who are the people or what are the situations at work that you envy?
- Are you lonely away from work?
- How does this sense of loneliness affect your performance? How aware are other people of how you feel?

# Ideas for action

## Examine critically your own sense of loneliness

Loneliness is an important but vague concept. The first thing you need to do is think about what makes up your loneliness. What are you missing? What do you feel you've lost? What do you need to replace? This will help you develop a specific understanding of your loneliness, allowing you to take steps to address each element of that loneliness.

If your sense of loneliness is recent or if you can pinpoint when it started to develop, look for what changed at about that time. Maybe new people joined the team or someone you really trusted left the team, changing the team dynamic; maybe the organisation's shape or structure changed; or maybe something changed for you at home. Try to identify the change that you can now associate with your growing feeling of loneliness. This will help you to decide how best to address that feeling.

Particularly if you've been promoted from within, you may find that the relationship with the people who used to be your teammates changes to something more formal and structured: the relationship between the manager and direct reports. You are no longer in a team with mates; you now know things you can't share with them and they know things they won't share with you. This is a difficult transition to manage, both for the manager and for the team members.

## Be aware of how others see you

As your career develops you need to remember that the more senior you are, and the more authority you have, the more important you are in the lives of the people in the organisation. The more authority you have, the harder it is for people to feel comfortable in a close relationship with you when they also have a reporting line to you. Even those without a direct reporting line to you may be wary of the amount of power you carry within the organisation.

## Recognise your role's potential for loneliness and isolation

Even if you haven't been promoted from within the team, loneliness and a sense of isolation is something every manager experiences to some extent as their management career develops. If you're not careful, the circle of people you can trust and be open with gets smaller and smaller. The trick is to look to source your friends from different places: make friends with other managers across the organisation rather than trying to do so with direct reports below you in the organis-ation. You'll find that the feelings of isolation you experience are probably the same as those they experience. The common ground of management is often enough to form the basis of a friendship which in time can grow into something that you both value.

## Build a pragmatic relationship with the people in your team

It's clearly important that managers have good relationships with the team they manage and with the individuals within the team. The thing to remember is that the nature of the relationship between manager and team or between manager and individuals is different in kind from the relationship between team members. This does not preclude the important need for the team to have a positive culture in which people, including you, feel involved, engaged and valued. Managers can't have favourites, can't exclude people, can't gossip, can't share information with some and not others – if you do any of these things you will find you rapidly lose the trust and respect of some or all of your team, at which point you will certainly become isolated and potentially lonely. Managers need to be open and honest but always professional in their behaviour.

## Remember to create and maintain a work–life balance

Make sure that your commitment to your career does not mean that you lose touch with friends outside work. Make an effort to keep in touch with people who like you and enjoy your company. Establish and maintain a network of friends who, like you, are professionals in a management role. These friends will understand the pressures you encounter and will experience them themselves, and are an invaluable source of support and objective advice. These relationships are also reciprocal: these friends will gain as much from you as you do from them.

At work, your mentor has an important role here. Your mentor may not be your friend necessarily (though mentors often become friends) but can certainly be your advisor and a listening ear.

## Recognise and accept your own level of need for relationships

Each of us has a different level of need for relationships. Some of us want lots of relationships in our lives, others have few but perhaps deeper relationships. Whatever your personal needs, if they are not being met, you will feel lonely and isolated. If these feelings are as true away from work as they are at work, then you should perhaps consider how you should change the pattern of your life to give you more opportunity to meet and form relationships with the types of people you like and admire. Remember that if you want people to include and involve you, you have to try to include and involve them in what you do. Relationships are two-way affairs.

# Having your authority or ability questioned

*None of us likes to have our authority or our ability challenged. Understanding the motivation for any such challenge will give you a framework for your response. Challenges such as these cannot go unanswered.*

## First, think:

- Is it possible that there is a legitimate reason for this challenge?
- Who is the person making the challenge? Is it a colleague, a team member or a superior? Is it someone outside the organisation?
- Is the challenger someone you respect? Are they motivated by self-interest or do they believe the challenge is necessary if the team is to meet its objectives?
- Is this a particularly difficult time for the team or for the organisation? Are emotions running high?
- How have you responded so far to the challenge?
- What is your status within the team? Within the organisation?
- How were you challenged? In a private conversation or in front of a group?
- Might you be reading too much into the situation?

## Ideas for action

### Relish fair challenges

Being in a management role means that you will be challenged, often appropriately, and often to the benefit of the team you are managing. So your first task is to decide whether this challenge is appropriate or inappropriate. When challenged you will have reacted to the culmination of a complex chain of events. If the person who has challenged you is someone with authority, whom you respect, who has spoken with you discreetly and privately, you may react in one way; if the challenge is overt, coming from somebody who probably has a hidden agenda and made in a public setting, you may react in another way.

As difficult as it might be, you must separate how you feel about being challenged from the validity of the challenge itself. Regardless of how you're challenged, if the challenger is making logical sense (and others can see that too) then what is being said must be acknowledged and then carefully examined. You will need to respond to the challenge, either accepting the criticism and agreeing to change, or rejecting it and explaining why you don't think it's appropriate. Depending on the nature of the challenge, it may be that 'business as usual' isn't possible until some resolution is achieved.

## Differentiate between public and private challenges

Generally speaking, a challenge made in private is less likely to be politically motivated and more likely to be grounded in genuine concern than one made in a public area. Challenges to your authority which are made not directly to you but through third parties or through the grapevine are insidious and are generally the work either of people who lack the courage to confront you or of people whose motivation is entirely political and mischievous. If you suspect such activity is taking place, you should gather evidence and then confront the individual in a private meeting. Your position will be strengthened if you can encourage people to confirm that this individual has been briefing against you. You can and should be quite stern, because this sort of behaviour will spread like poison and quickly undermine your authority and the team's culture.

## Consider carefully the context in which a challenge is made

Context is extremely important. Challenges to your authority or competence must be framed within an understanding of variables such as your status within the team or organisation, the respect in which you are held and your level of experience. Your challenger may be someone who wanted your job and is bitter. Or it may be a newcomer to the team who believes you can be usurped. The important thing is to analyse your particular circumstance so that you have a full grasp of the challenge which is taking place.

Sometimes a challenge to your authority or competence is more of a signal of discontent or frustration or dissatisfaction. Such a signal can often be sent in times of turmoil, sudden or unexpected change, or business or economic pressures. You need to be sensitive to these signals and make sure that you deal with the underlying cause rather than focus simply on the signal of the challenge.

If the person who is challenging you is senior to you in the organisation, you must first try to establish why you are being challenged. Do you represent a threat? Are you holding a position this individual wants to give to one of their own supporters? Does this individual's reputation depend to some extent on your performance? Generally there are specific reasons behind such attacks, though occasionally someone may simply be so cross-grained that this sort of behaviour is entirely normal for them. Understanding the reasons behind the challenge will help you to decide the best course of action. If you have a wide network of influencers within the organisation who are able to support you, be sure to engage with them. Your boss may be able to support you, but before you approach him or her you must be sure that there is no substance in the challenge.

## Treat challenges from externals differently

Dealing with this type of challenge from an external source (a client, a customer or a supplier) is different. Understanding why they are challenging you remains important: are they concerned about your stance and the ramifications it has on their business or their budgets? Did they have a particularly close relationship with the person who held this position before you? Is there somebody they would prefer to see in the position now? The difficulty you face is that the politics are more overt and often more important when the challenger is giving business to the organisation. Senior people are likely to be involved more quickly and their priority will always be the impact on the business rather than on you. In this context you need constantly to think about the degree of support you are likely to get as you decide how best to address the challenge. The overall effect of external challenges is that you are often disempowered, regardless of whether or not the challenge made is valid.

## Decide whether there is a long-term intention to undermine you

Not every challenge is an overt single event. Often, people will attempt to undermine your position or your competence over a protracted period of time and in a subtle, even sly way. This sort of challenge is much harder to combat. The risk to you is that you will appear to be defensive and over-reacting because others are not aware of the constant, subtle attacks on you. They will only see the small incident to which your response may seem disproportionate.

In such a case your best option is to seek a private meeting with the person who you believe is undermining you. Making sure you are well armed with examples, you need to make it clear that you are aware of what is happening and are determined to make it stop. If this approach does not work, your two choices are then either to elevate the issue, involving more senior management, or to be as well prepared as possible for likely continuing attacks during meetings. At these meetings you must be seen as being firm but fair in your responses. Keep your tone assertive and professional; do not allow this to become a personal battle.

## Don't duck!

The sorts of challenges we describe here are an inevitable part of a manager's life. You will need courage and resilience to face them, coupled with a thick skin. The most important thing for you to do is to understand the context in which the challenge is being made and the motivation of the person making the challenge. This will help you to deal with the situation in the most appropriate way.

# Asking for a raise or promotion

*Managers often feel that asking for a pay raise or promotion should not be something they have to do; their work speaks for itself and the reward and recognition that goes with doing their job well should come to them rather than be something they have to pursue. Nevertheless, career-minded managers also often feel that they have as much responsibility for managing their career as their employers.*

## First, think:

- Do you have a strong business case for this request? Is the case strong enough to match the performance and achievements of individuals who are currently at the level to which you aspire?
- What is the system within your organisation? Is it well defined and properly followed?
- Is your organisation the equivalent of a free-market economy? Is it up to you to demonstrate your worth and then to set about obtaining it? What is an equivalent role worth elsewhere?
- Who is responsible for the final decision? Is it your boss or a team of people? Whose support do you already have?
- Are you assertive enough to pursue what you want with confidence?
- What happens if you don't succeed in getting this promotion or raise? How will you be seen internally and how will you feel about that result?

- Consider management's position: would getting what you want open floodgates or set precedents?

# Ideas for action

## Preparation is key

You must have a thoughtful, justified business case which is clear and airtight. The business case must be based on something more than your own sense of ambition and self-worth. You must also understand the likely position and response of management. Sometimes, however much you deserve a raise or promotion, the funds or the position are simply not available. Management must also consider the impact of whatever they give you on others in the organisation.

If you do decide to go for meeting to discuss a promotion or raise, you must plan both what you want and how you will ask for it. Be prepared for the best-case and worst-case scenarios. Above all, don't go into the meeting threatening to leave unless you really mean it. The trouble with offering ultimatums is that, at best, if they are accepted there is a lingering sense of resentment and, at worst, you are taken at your word.

## Ask, don't demand

Often the best way to approach negotiations around pay and position is to ask questions first about the organisation's view on you, your future and your potential within the organisation. It might be that what you want is just around the corner, and waiting for it to arrive is better for you than demanding it now. Equally, if the organisation has a very different view of your future than you have, you may decide that asking for a raise or promotion is a futile exercise and what you need to do is find an organisation whose sense of your ability is more aligned to your own.

In many organisations there are salary bands and movement to a higher band is subject to specific and measurable criteria which are assessed by a team of people. In this type of organisation there is a clear and formal process to follow and there is very little to be gained by trying to buck the system. In smaller or more informal organisations, it's more appropriate to ask for what you believe you deserve, because there is no structured system in place. Here you will need to influence and negotiate your way to a better package. For some managers this can be a very stressful system within which to operate.

## Differentiate between reward and responsibility

Bear in mind that there is a difference between asking your organisation for more money and asking for more responsibility. A new title or new responsibilities at the same salary is often a more palatable proposition for management to consider. Perhaps you can agree in advance that your salary will be reviewed after six months in post. Once you have proved yourself in this new role then asking for more money is easier.

## Get some support

Part of making your case for a raise should be seeking senior people who are prepared to champion your cause. Being able to say in your meeting that the head of another department believes your case to be deserving can be a significant influencer. It's even better if these champions can have a quiet word on your behalf before the meeting takes place. If you find it difficult to recruit such champions, it may be that your case is not as strong as you might believe.

Remember that if you don't get what you want you should not act in haste. Be calm and bear in mind that your organisation does not need to know that you are carefully considering your position and your options. Carry on as normal while looking for ways to develop your career elsewhere within the organisation or outside it. Being a bad loser, especially if that means complaining to other people about your treatment, will win you no respect among the decision makers and will probably undermine your chances of future success. If you feel so strongly that you will leave if you do not get what you want, you should either have something lined up to go to or accept the decision gracefully and then seek a new position. This allows you to leave on your own terms.

## If you are not sure about the answer, think hard before asking the question

Properly done, asking for a raise or a promotion should not be traumatic. Ideally you should be in very little doubt that the outcome will be positive before you enter the meeting. The worst-case scenario should be that you leave the meeting with a very clear sense of where and how you need to improve in order to get the promotion or raise you want. Try to get a timescale around this and an agreement that meeting the targets agreed will lead to a salary increase and/or a change of position.

# Index

# Take your skills to another level

with these three essential management guides
from the award-winning expert, Jo Owen

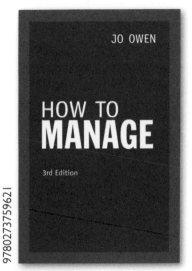

JO OWEN

**HOW TO**
**MANAGE**

3rd Edition

9780273759621

JO OWEN

**HOW TO**
**LEAD**

3rd Edition

9780273759614

JO OWEN

**HOW TO**
**COACH**
Coaching yourself and
your team to success

9780273786382